Nuptial Favors

Nuptial Favors

Assorted Scenarios

KEN BAZYN

RESOURCE *Publications* • Eugene, Oregon

NUPTIAL FAVORS
Assorted Scenarios

Copyright © 2020 Ken Bazyn. All rights reserved. Except for brief quotations in critical publications or reviews, no part of this book may be reproduced in any manner without prior written permission from the publisher. Write: Permissions, Wipf and Stock Publishers, 199 W. 8th Ave., Suite 3, Eugene, OR 97401.

New Revised Standard Version Bible, copyright 1989, Division of Christian Education of the National Council of Churches of Christ in the United States of America. Used by permission. All rights reserved.

Resource Publications
An Imprint of Wipf and Stock Publishers
199 W. 8th Ave., Suite 3
Eugene, OR 97401

www.wipfandstock.com

PAPERBACK ISBN: 978-1-7252-6057-3
HARDCOVER ISBN: 978-1-7252-6055-9
EBOOK ISBN: 978-1-7252-6056-6

Manufactured in the U.S.A. 04/03/20

Contents

Acknowledgments   ix
*Introduction: The Language and
   Imagery of Song of Songs*   xi

I. Tongue in Cheek

An Old, Crinkled Treasure Chest   2
A Valentine   4
Love's Rags   6
. . . how much I love you?   8
The Abduction   10
Lay Siege to a Maiden's Honor   12
Outside Your Door   14
Good Juliet   17
Some Loving Potion   20
Determined Lovers   22
The Song of the Young Brave   25
To Please My Friend   27

II. Marital Woes

After a Hell-Raising   29
Critical Likeness   31

Why Don't You Listen?	33
Go Away and Nest Elsewhere?	35
Last Night	37
Of a St. Agnes' Night	39
Scamper Away Now, Phoebus	41
Either This or That	44
The Wind Has Turned	46
The Music Box	48
M	50
Tears Are Outlawed	52
The Imprint of Love	54
The Keepsake	56
A 25-Year-Old Menopause Man	58

III. A Child, Too

My Flaming Meteor	60
How Do They Come?	62
Baby's Playpen	65
A Child's Declaration of Rights	67
The World According to Da-da	69
When You're 30	72
My Frenetic Nerves	75
Hush You, Chil'!	77

IV. A Classical Interlude

Giving Birth	80
The Judgment of Paris	82
Penelope	85
Echo, the Nymph	87
Venus	89
Medea with her Medusa Head	91

V. Scriptural Illumination

Abram's Quandary	93
Hosea	96
The foolish virgins	98
A la John of the Cross	100
Two Nude Virgins	102
a *Charis* all can partake of	104

VI. Au Naturel

Au Naturel	106
Satisfying a Poet	108
Near Dejection	110
The Stone Woman	112
Erotic Architecture	114
You, a Gazelle	116
Nakedness in the Morning	118
Mermaids on Land?	120

VII. Outside Proper Boundaries

The Hollow Suburbs	122
Keep Away from Knives	124
She Entered the Blue, Virginal Sky	126
Promiscuity	128
Love's Laissez-Faire Dilettante	130
An Old West Advertisement	132

| *Listing of Photographs* | 133 |
| *Works Cited* | 137 |

Acknowledgments

It is with due appreciation that I mention how numerous were the concrete suggestions concerning grammar, style, and substance given by my wife, Barbara. She has been aided by the able and diligent hand of David Reynolds, who with a fine-tooth comb oversaw the formatting and final text.

Wipf & Stock continues to expand their fine line of outstanding Christian poetry—something we all can be grateful for. I'd also like to recognize Savanah Landerholm for her fine typesetting gifts, Robert Meier for hand-developing my b&w film, and Rockbrook Camera in Omaha for reproducing my 35 mm negatives onto a superb CD.

Thanks to these magazines for being the first to run the following poems:

"Love's Rags" in *Forum*
"Go Away and Nest Elsewhere?" in *Earthwise*
"Au Naturel" in *Harpoon*

Introduction
The Language and Imagery of Song of Songs

It may come as a surprise to the average layperson that the Bible contains rather moving love poetry. I'm referring, of course, to Song of Songs, which is filled with spiritually influential, as well as exotic, metaphors and similes. Since the publication of *Lieder der Liebe* by the German philosopher Johann Gottfried von Herder in 1778,[1] scholars have generally come to see the book as a series of lyric poems loosely tied together. Closely related to ancient Egyptian love songs which may date from roughly the same period, these poems should be interpreted in a straightforward sense.[2]

Though Theodore of Mopsuestia (c. AD 350–428) advocated a literal understanding of Songs of Songs, the popularity of the allegorical approach was so strong that such views were virtually ignored for centuries.[3] Only in the 1560s did the highly-regarded Spanish monk Luis de Leon compose his own original translation directly from the Hebrew, treating the text as if it were a pastoral poem.[4] So, it is with some justification that Sue Brideshead, in Hardy's *Jude the Obscure*, complains, "I *hate* such humbug as could attempt to plaster over with ecclesiastical abstractions such ecstatic, natural, human love as lies in that great and passionate song."[5] Let's, instead, try to make sense of the language and imagery of Song of Songs, which, on occasion, seems strange to modern ears.

1. Herder, *Lieder der Liebe*.

2. Foster, "Love Poetry, Egyptian," 169. There are four small collections totaling about 60 poems from the Ramesside period of the New Kingdom (ca. 1305–1080 B.C.).

3. Greer, *Theodore of Mopsuestia*, 86–131.

4. Nahson, *Song of Songs: Fray Luis de Leon's Spanish translation*.

5. Hardy, *Jude the Obscure*, 160.

Introduction

Despite numerous attempts by commentators over the centuries, it has proven difficult to discern an overall plot or narrative in the book, nor does it appear to be an actual drama, although there are several voices, including at least one male and one female. There is an ongoing dialogue between the lovers, as well as startling visual catalogs of the beloved's features (sometimes referred to as *wasfs*, the Arab word for "descriptions"), a deep yearning for togetherness, and invitations to rendezvous. While sensual and suggestive, the verses are not crude or offensive. Goethe called the book the most tender and inimitable expression of passionate, yet graceful, love that has come down to us, although he thought the verses fragmentary, telescoped or driven into one another, and rather mixed up.[6] In later Judaism, some of these lyrics would be turned into wedding songs.

Those who want to allegorize the book have yet to show an obvious one-to-one correspondence between God and Israel (or the church) within the text, or even much reference to deity. And contrary to popular belief, Solomon is neither a speaker nor a principal character in the Song, though his name does appear six times; he seems, instead, a literary prop meant to create poetic contrast.[7] Even within the lovers' speeches, it's not easy to distinguish what's really happening from what's being imagined, with sections 3:1–5 and 5:2–8 often considered to be dreams.

The book's setting appears to be Jerusalem and its outlying environs, the time of year spring, when all is in bloom. For background, it's important to remember that, in the Book of Genesis, God deemed all of creation "good," including the first man and woman. Eve, taken from Adam's rib, was meant to be his intimate companion; upon seeing her, he exclaimed, "bone of my bones and flesh of my flesh" (2:23). The norm, ever since, has been for a man to leave his father and mother and cleave to his wife, becoming "one flesh" with her (2:24). The initial couple were told to "be fruitful and multiply," that is, to have offspring (1:28). *Yada*, a common Old Testament Hebrew verb translated as "to know," can mean engaging in sex, learning new things about the body and personality of one's partner (Gen. 4:1,17, 25).[8] In Song of Songs, the Hebrew word *dodim* occurs six times (1:2; 1:4; 4:10; 4:10; 5:1; 7:12); it is usually translated simply as "love," but it actually refers to sexual love.[9] In ancient Israel, lovemaking was regarded

---

6. Haupt, *Book of Canticles*, 18.
7. Falk, *Song of Songs*, 166.
8. Ryken, et al., "Sex," 778.
9. Bloch and Bloch, *Song of Songs*, 3.

as something marvelous and a cause for celebration. "Three things are too wonderful for me; four I do not understand," declares the Book of Proverbs (30:18–19), "the way of an eagle in the sky, the way of a snake on a rock, the way of a ship on the high seas, and the way of a man with a girl."

Karl Barth, in *Church Dogmatics*, called Genesis 2:18–25 the "Old Testament Magna Carta of humanity." "It is not good that the man should be alone," according to Genesis 2:18; he needs a partner. Barth observes, "God did not create man . . . as a single human being, but in the unequal duality of male and female."[10] In that key verse (1:26), the plural is used for both God and man: "Let us make humankind in our image." Since God isn't solitary (Christians regard him as a Trinity), neither should the capstone of his creation be. "Man is directed to woman and woman to man," notes Barth, "each being for the other a horizon and focus."[11] He goes on to regard Song of Songs as a "second Magna Carta," since it fills out that relationship between man and woman so briefly sketched in by Genesis 2.[12] Song of Songs, in his view, is "one long description of the rapture, the unquenchable yearning and the restless willingness and readiness, with which both partners in this covenant hasten towards an encounter."[13]

The poems present a portrait of the two sexes in love, just as God intended. American psychologist Abraham Maslow, famous for his hierarchy of needs and the self-actualizing personality, describes this ideal: Love "consists primarily of a feeling of tenderness and affection with great enjoyment, happiness, and satisfaction . . . There is a tendency to want to get closer, to come into more intimate contact, to touch and embrace the loved person, to yearn for him." The beloved, adds Maslow, is seen to be "desirable," whether "beautiful," "good," or "attractive." Moreover, "there is pleasure in looking at and being with the loved one and distress in separation."[14] "The healthy love relationship," he concludes, "is the most effective way of bridging the unbridgeable gap between two separate beings."[15]

"Rejoice in the wife of your youth, a lovely deer, a graceful doe," the Book of Proverbs advises (5:18–19): "May her breasts satisfy you at all times; may you be intoxicated always by her love." "Enjoy life with the wife

---

10. Barth, *Church Dogmatics*, III.1, 288.
11. Barth, *Church Dogmatics*, III.4, 163.
12. Murphy, *Song of Songs*, 100.
13. Barth, *Church Dogmatics*, III.1, 313.
14. Maslow, "Love in Healthy People," 91–92.
15. Maslow, "Love in Healthy People," 103.

INTRODUCTION

whom you love, all the days of our vain life," recommends Ecclesiastes 9:9. "Be drunk with love" (5:1), urges Song of Songs, for kisses are sweeter than wine (1:2). An ancient Egyptian love poem in a similar manner relates, "Her lips open wide as I kiss her,/And I rejoice (even) without beer."[16] "Caress the breasts of the lovely girl at night, and kiss the lips of the beautiful girl all day long!" medieval Jewish poet Moses Ibn Ezra exclaims. Then, in a playful reference to the Hebrew sacrifice at the ordination of the priests of Aaron (Exod. 29:26–27), he adds, "Do not stop sipping the moist lips until you hold your rightful portion—the breast and the thigh!"[17]

"Love is strong as death,/passion fierce as the grave," confirms Song 8:6–7. "Its flashes are flashes of fire,/a raging flame./Many waters cannot quench love,/neither can floods drown it." Consider the great lovers in literature: Paris and Helen, Isaac and Rebekah, Pyramus and Thisbe, Daphnis and Chloe, Layla and Majnun, Tristan and Iseult, Guinevere and Lancelot, Romeo and Juliet, etc. So ardent is their passion that curfews, threats, walls, and banishment cannot hold two determined souls apart for long. As the Roman poet Tibullus puts it, "Love laughs at locksmiths."[18] To fall in love, posits C.S. Lewis, means that we have "overleaped the massive wall of our own selfhood" and "planted the interests of another at the center of our being."[19] As the beloved in Song of Songs cries out, "Take me by the hand, let us run together!" (1:4).[20] Eros is one of the most powerful of human emotions, yet, if mishandled, it can lead to anguish and heartache, even violence.

How frequently do lovers meet in a pastoral setting in world literature (e.g. Gen. 29:9–14; Exod. 2:15–22; Song 1:7–8). Not surprisingly then, the most common imagery is drawn from nature (e.g. 4:1–7; 5:10–16; 6:4–7; 7:1–5). Even today, we hear people speak of sex in terms of "the birds and the bees." Song of Songs is filled with allusions to flowers (henna, wild rose, lily, grape and fig blossoms), trees (pine, cedar, apple, and palm), agricultural products (raisins, nuts, pomegranates, dates, figs, wheat, wine, and honey), and animals (gazelle, stag, turtledove, sheep, and horse).[21]

---

16. Simpson, *Literature of Ancient Egypt*, 3rd. ed., 318.
17. Carmi, *Penguin Book of Hebrew Verse*, 324–25.
18. Carrier, *Poems of Tibullus*, 36.
19. Lewis, *Four Loves*, 158.
20. Bloch and Bloch, *Song of Songs*, 45.
21. Gottwald, "Song of Songs," 425.

INTRODUCTION

Though the meanings of the more obscure Hebrew words in Song of Songs are debatable (there are perhaps forty-six unique to this book), as are some of the Egyptian words in the translations I refer to, I'll do my best to investigate their import. "I am black and beautiful," the Shulammite maiden proclaims (1:5), referring to her peasant suntan (1:6). She coyly hides from her lover, like a dove nesting in the clefts of the rock (2:14). The male is likened to a gazelle or a young stag (2:9). He comes leaping down from the hills and stands outside the house peering in through the window.[22] In an ancient Egyptian poem, the male also is referred to as "a gazelle bounding across the desert/Its feet move swiftly."[23] In Song of Songs, the male stands out as distinct as an apple tree in a thicket (2:3), much as in a Sumerian poem where the lover is praised as "my apple tree that bears fruit up to its crown."[24]

Even celestial phenomena come into play, as the male inquires, "Who is that rising like the morning star?" then describes his beloved as "clear as the moon, bright as the blazing sun, daunting as the stars in their courses!" (6:10)[25] How close this is to an ancient Egyptian poem, where the beloved is a "star which appears/At the onset of a prosperous year."[26]

Throughout Song of Songs there is double entendre and euphemism. The female is portrayed as a garden filled with gentle breezes and fragrant flowers, watered by a hidden spring (4:12–16).[27] She beckons, "Let my beloved come to his garden/and eat its choicest fruits" (4:16). Emphasis is placed upon sweetness—tasting honey and honeycomb (5:1); honey and milk on one's tongue (4:11). "Strengthen me with raisin cakes/refresh me with apples" (2:5), she remarks.[28] As stately as a palm she stands (7:7)! What should one do then, but climb up and enjoy her dates (7:8)?[29] Neo-Assyrian lyrics concerning the deities Nabu and Tashmetu display comparable images: her thighs are as "a gazelle in the steppe . . . ankles are a springtime

---

22. Alter, *Strong as Death*, 16–17.
23. Simpson, *Literature of Ancient Egypt*, 3rd. ed., 328.
24. Keel, *Song of Songs*, 82.
25. Bloch and Bloch, *Song of Songs*, 95.
26. Simpson, *Literature of Ancient Egypt*, 3rd. ed., 322.
27. Alter, *Art of Biblical Poetry*, 197, 202.
28. Murphy, *Song of Songs*, 130.
29. Keel, *Song of Songs*, 245. A relief from the ninth century BC shows a man climbing a ladder, either to pollinate a stylized palm or to harvest its fruit.

Introduction

apple... she washes herself, she climbs into bed... Why are you so adorned, Tashmetu? So I can go to the garden with you, my Nabu."[30]

Song of Songs describes no ordinary garden, for here grow "flowering henna and spikenard,/spikenard and saffron, cane and cinnamon,/with every tree of frankincense,/myrrh and aloes,/all the rare spices" (4:13–14).[31] While botanists believe henna and saffron could be found in ancient Israel, myrrh, cinnamon, and cane probably could not—and frankincense, aloes, and spikenard were likely luxury imports from such faraway places as Arabia, India, and China. The garden pictured here is a lover's idealized fantasy.[32]

Every sense is invoked in the couple's deepening relationship, as they respond to taste (2:3; 4:11; 5:1), touch (7:6–9), smell (1:12–14; 4:16), and the sound of each other's voices (2:8,14; 5:16).[33] "It is pomegranate wine to hear your voice,/And I live (only) to hear it," an Egyptian lyric similarly states.[34] The female desires that the male be placed as a sachet of fragrances between her breasts (1:13) or a cluster of henna pressed against her body (1:14).[35] Her tresses are enticing enough to capture a king (7:5). Likewise, an ancient Egyptian quips, "With her hair she throws lassos at me."[36] Furthermore, the female's figure is enhanced by her necklace and jewelry (1:10–11).

In the great Western tradition of love poetry, Andrew Marvell draws on such imagery in "To His Coy Mistress," in which the lover/narrator complains of not having "world enough, and time" to fully savor his beloved, desiring a hundred years to praise her eyes, two hundred for each breast, concluding, "Let us sport while we may/... like amorous birds of prey."[37] In "The Garden," ripe apples, luscious clusters of the vine, the nectarine, the curious peach, and melons are his simply for the taking.[38] Such fruit allures and ensnares. "All these eatable beauties," notes literary critic William Empson, "give themselves so as to lose themselves, like a lover, with a forceful generosity."[39]

30. Foster, *Before the Muses*, 903. Cf. Long, "Song of Songs," 758.
31. Bloch and Bloch, *Song of Songs*, 79.
32. Bloch and Bloch, *Song of Songs*, 8.
33. Weems, "Song of Songs," 158.
34. Simpson, *Literature of Ancient Egypt*, 3rd. ed., 316.
35. Alter, *Strong as Death*, 11–12.
36. Simpson, *Literature of Ancient Egypt*, New ed., 324.
37. Stallsworthy, *Penguin Book of Love Poetry*, 80–82.
38. Gardner, *Metaphysical Poets*, 255–58.
39. Empson, *Some Versions of Pastoral*, 126.

Introduction

"Green" is a key word in the poem; indeed, all of life eventually collapses into "a green thought in a green shade."[40] The poem's theme is repose. As Marvell noted elsewhere, "The pleasures of the country give a repose and intellectual release which make me less intellectual, make my mind less worrying and introspective."[41] So too do the lovers in Song of Songs create an alternate universe, oblivious to the turmoil of the outside world.

The male and female make love on the forest floor (1:16–17).[42] She offers to visit him wherever he pastures his flock (1:7); she invites him to go into the fields (7:12). An infatuated ancient Egyptian also confesses, "(How) pleasant it is for one who is cherished to go to the fields."[43] One thinks of that amusing Egyptian song where three different trees discuss the goings-on under their leaves and branches, with only the little sycamore discreet enough not to reveal its secrets.[44] The medieval German minnesinger Walther von der Vogelweide mentions one such tryst in a poem: "Under the linden/on the heath/there was the bed for the two of us,/there you can find/two beautiful broken things:/flowers and grass."[45] The female in Song of Songs recalls how she had once tended another's vineyard, but now, sorry to say, she had not taken care of her own (that is, her virginity), much to her brothers' chagrin (1:6).

The sexual imagery encompasses city life as well: latches, towers and walls, inner chambers. "My lover thrust his hand through the latch opening;/my heart began to pound for him./I arose to open to my lover" (5:4–5 NIV). An ancient Egyptian recounts, "I knocked, but no one opened to me./Perhaps the doorkeeper was enjoying a good night's sleep!"[46] In Song of Songs, the female's breasts appear like towers. In the first half of the verse she likens herself to a wall which can serve as a line of defense in time of war. These towers and this wall had withstood all assault until now. But she had handed them over of her own free will to her lover: "I was a wall/and my breasts were like towers;/then I became to him/like a surrendered city"

---

40. Empson, *Some Versions of Pastoral*, 121.
41. Empson, *Some Versions of Pastoral*, 117, 119
42. Alter, *Strong as Death*, 12.
43. Simpson, *Literature of Ancient Egypt*, 3rd. ed., 312.
44. Simpson, *Literature of Ancient Egypt*, 3rd. ed., 319–22.
45. Keel, *Song of Songs*, 76. Cf. Foster, *Penguin Book of German Verse*, 23–24.
46. Simpson, *Literature of Ancient Egypt*, 3rd. ed., 331.

INTRODUCTION

(8:10).[47] Elsewhere she pulls her lover into the secluded chambers of her mother's house (3:4).

Some see "calvary," "infantry," or "a fleet of long oars" as "the supreme sight on the black earth," the ancient Greek lyricist Sappho famously announces in "To Anaktoria," before adding "I say it is/the one you love."[48] Song of Songs contains four visual catalogues praising the beloved's features, three of the woman and one of the man (4:1–7; 5:10–16; 6:4–10; 7:1–7). In chapter 7, verses 1–7, we hear how the dancing Shulammite has curving thighs like jewels, a navel like a rounded bowl, a belly like a heap of wheat; her two breasts resemble two fawns; her neck is like an ivory tower (in the ancient Near East long necks were considered beautiful—think of Nefertiti),[49] her eyes like the pools of Heshbon, her nose like a tower of Lebanon, her head majestic as Mount Carmel.[50] These aren't meant to be realistic descriptions, but help to set a mood. In every culture, beauty is in the eyes of the beholder. My beloved is unequalled in beauty, writes an Egyptian counterpart: with radiant eyes, lips sweet in speaking, a high neck, "resplendent" breasts, "lapis lazuli" hair, "lotus flower" fingers, a slender waist. It's charming just to watch her walk.[51]

In contrast with feminine images, frequently drawn from the flora, fauna, or landscape, the masculine images (5:10–16) appear more architectural and sculptural, displaying a statue-like hardness (5:14).[52] The male's head is compared to finest gold, his arms to gold coils inset with jewels. His body is like ivory work decorated with sapphires. His legs are alabaster columns set upon bases of gold. He is attractive, yes, even stunning. Ramses III is praised by an Egyptian princess, "Your hair [is] lapis lazuli, your eyebrows [are] stone, your eyes [are] green malachite, your mouth [is] red jasper."[53]

Images which are stranger still to modern listeners include hair like a flock of goats, teeth like newly washed ewes, none of which are bereaved (6:5–6)—the latter capturing such qualities as whiteness, moistness,

47. Boman, *Hebrew Thought Compared with Greek*, 77–78.
48. Barnstone, *Greek Lyric Poetry*, 66.
49. Kahane, *20,000 Years of World Painting*, Vol. 1, 65.
50. Alter, *Art of Biblical Poetry*, 196.
51. Simpson, *Literature of Ancient Egypt*, 3rd. ed., 322–23.
52. Alter, *Strong as Death*, 34. There are obvious exceptions, as when the female is compared to the cities of Tirzah and Jerusalem, or to an army with banners (6:4).
53. Keel, *Song of Songs*, 203.

symmetry, lack of flaws.[54] Recall similarly odd comparisons in metaphysical verse—lovers like two stiff legs of a compass in Donne's "A Valediction: Forbidding Mourning" or Mary Magdalene's tears as "two faithful fountains;/Two walking baths; two weeping motions;/Portable, and compendious oceans" in "The Weeper" by Crashaw.[55] And what of the beloved's cheeks behind the veil, compared to a slice of a pomegranate (6:7)? This may seem puzzling at first, but it could just depict how rosy skin is glimpsed through white netting.[56] Poets are ever torn between the desire to startle and to be colloquial,[57] that longing to be both paradoxical and coherent.

The male is particularly fond of affectionate epithets: "my love," "my friend," "my sister, my bride," "my dove," "my perfect one."[58] What is especially endearing is the intensity of the relationship between the man and woman (the female actually has more lines than the male). There is coquetry or flirtation, lovesickness and fear of loss, sensuous longing as well as consummation.[59] One discovers a lovers' game of hide-and-seek.[60] Each looks anxiously for the other; he issues an invitation, then tries to find her; she calls, then seeks him out.

Sometimes, though, it is difficult to follow the flow of the dialogue, or even to know who actually is speaking. The feelings of the two are mutual; even the metaphors and phrases can be parallel. Readers are eager to follow the response and counter-response, to hear the verbal echoes. He describes her as a garden of spices (4:12–15); she picks up on the hint and urges him to come visit (4:16); he accepts wholeheartedly (5:1). She refers to herself modestly as a crocus of Sharon; no, he asserts, she stands out like a lily among brambles; she, in turn, considers him as distinct as an apple tree in a thicket (2:1–3). There is deep admiration between the two (and not a little flattery): he claims her lips drip nectar (4:11); she says that his distill liquid myrrh (5:13). She considers his love sweeter than wine and, oh, how delightful his fragrance (1:2–3); he later returns the favor (4:10).[61] He is as enchanted by her beauty as she is by his (1:15–16). The couple

54. Ryken, et al., "Song of Songs," 807.
55. Falk, *Song of Songs*, 128–29.
56. Falk, *Song of Songs*, 131.
57. Grierson, "Metaphysical Poetry," 10.
58. Bloch and Bloch, *Song of Songs*, 8.
59. Gottwald, "Song of Songs," 425.
60. Falk, *Song of Songs*, 119.
61. Fox, *Song of Songs and Ancient Egyptian Love Songs*, 315–22.

INTRODUCTION

seems as joyous and contrapuntal as Papageno and Papagena in Mozart's *Magic Flute*.[62]

In the final chapter of Song of Songs, the beloved urges, "Bind me as a seal upon your heart, a sign upon your arm" (8:6), desiring that the two remain true to each other forever. Such a seal implies physical closeness, intimacy, and belonging. Seals or signets, made of metal or stone, often exquisitely engraved, would be worn on the finger as a ring, on the arm as an amulet, or around the head in the form of a necklace.[63] "With her eyes she entraps me,/With her necklace she binds me," an ancient Egyptian observes, "And with her signet ring she brands me."[64] In cultures around the world, lovers have often worn some item to identify them with the beloved.[65] Finally, Song of Songs insists that love can't be bought; it must be given freely (8:7).

"It seems clear," psychologist Abraham Maslow writes, "that healthy people fall in love the way one reacts to one's first appreciative perception of great music—one is awed and overwhelmed."[66] Chastity isn't what's on display in Song of Songs, but devotion to one's lover.[67] They desire exclusivity, a relationship in which the beloved is not shared with anyone (8:11–12). That repeated phrase, "My beloved is mine and I am his;/he pastures his flock among the lilies" (2:16; cf. 6:3; 7:10) points to togetherness and contentment.[68] This is that kind of love which, as John Donne in "The Ecstasy" says, "interanimates two souls."[69] The lovers' reciprocity has even been compared to Buber's I-Thou relationship.[70]

What's *not* on display in The Song of Songs? There is no love-at-first-sight or swooning at the beloved as in ancient Greek romances like Xenophon of Ephesus.[71] Nor is love depicted as some all-consuming disease, as in Sappho, where it is accompanied by fluttering heartbeats, burning

---

62. Lewis, *Four Loves*, 141.
63. Bloch and Bloch, *Song of Songs*, 5, 111, 212.
64. Simpson, *Literature of Ancient Egypt*, 3rd. ed., 330.
65. Murphy, *Song of Songs*, 191.
66. Maslow, "Love in Healthy People," 107.
67. Fox, *Song of Songs and Ancient Egyptian Love Songs*, 315.
68. Murphy, *Song of Songs*, 139.
69. Stallsworthy, *Penguin Book of Love Poetry*, 150. Cf. Fox, *Song of Songs and Ancient Love Songs*, 322.
70. Falk, *Song of Songs*, 119.
71. Hadas, *Three Greek Romances*.

INTRODUCTION

sensations, cold sweats, paleness, and trembling.[72] There are no midnight pickups or partying as in Catullus, nor explicit advice and stratagems for finding and keeping a lover as in Ovid.[73] The lovers do not yearn for their one and only true counterpart as in the myth of Aristophanes in Plato's *Symposium*.[74] Nor does one find dark plot complications as in Romeo and Juliet or Tristan and Iseult. Sex is not glorified as the quintessence of life as in Walt Whitman's "Children of Adam."[75] Nor is love a form of cosmic merger as in the Tantric schools of Hinduism and Buddhism, where "the jewel" is said to be "in the lotus."[76] We find no medieval courtly love in which eternal pursuit is more enthralling than actual possession.[77] Nor, strangely enough, are there any warnings of the havoc an overheated libido can wreak, as seen in those telltale images of a blindfolded Cupid, firing arrows in all directions.[78]

Still, it's not surprising that an allegorical reading arose concerning Song of Songs, since piety and sensuality have much in common, i.e., a desire for intimacy and self-abandonment.[79] "As a deer longs for flowing streams, so my soul longs for you, O God," pants the Psalmist (42:1). Beauty ever draws us to God even from this world's poor facsimiles. "But, my God and my glory, for this reason I say a hymn of praise to you," intoned Augustine. "For the beautiful objects designed by artists' souls and realized by skilled hands come from that beauty which is higher than souls; after that beauty my soul sighs day and night."[80] In "The Good-Morrow" Donne confesses concerning his wife, Anne More, "If ever any beauty I did see,/ Which I desir'd, and got, 'twas but a dreame of thee."[81] Such beauty lifts us upward like Beatrice in Dante's *The Divine Comedy* or Laura in Petrarch's

---

72. Bloch and Bloch, *Song of* Songs, 7. Cf. Barnstone, *Greek Lyric Poetry*, 67–68 (e.g., "Seizure").

73. Paglia, "Love Poetry: Western," 165–66.

74. Plato, *Dialogues of Plato*, Vol. 1, 559–63. Cf. Lewis, *Four Loves*, 152.

75. Whitman, *Complete Poetry and Selected Prose*, 69–83 (e.g., "A Woman Waits for Me").

76. Tannahill, *Sex in History*, 223–24.

77. De Rougemont, *Love in the Western World*, 284.

78. Mace, *Marriage: East & West*, 132.

79. Scheindlin, *Gazelle*, 40.

80. Augustine, *Confessions*, 210.

81. Gardner, *Metaphysical Poets*, 58.

Introduction

verse. "The earth has grown light," an ancient Egyptian sighs, due to the "beauty" of his beloved.[82]

Biblical analogies are certainly there: God did take Israel as his wife (Isa. 62:4-5; Ezekiel chapters 16, 23; Hosea). "What is that coming up from the wilderness,/like a column of smoke,/perfumed with myrrh and frankincense,/with all the fragrant powders of the merchant?" asks Song of Songs (3:6). The Targum answers that it is Israel. The question is repeated again in 8:5: "Who is that coming up from the wilderness,/leaning upon her beloved?"[83] Traditionally, the beloved's breasts (1:13) were understood to represent the two golden cherubim which stood on the ark in the Holy of Holies or the two poles which carried the ark in the desert.[84] Any allegorical reading, however, loses that delicious mutuality, that playful tête-à-tête in the Song of Songs, for how can God ever be an equal partner in marriage?

Jesus employed the metaphor of bride and bridegroom for his relationship to the disciples (Matt. 9:15; 25:1-13); Paul saw the church as the bride of Christ (Eph. 5:21-33), as did John in the Apocalypse (Rev. 21:9—22:5). Bernard of Clairvaux famously produced 86 allegorical sermons on just the first two chapters of Song of Songs. In *Quia Amore Langueo*, a fifteenth-century poet hears the words from Song of Songs 2:5 (and 5:8) as though spoken by Jesus from the cross to sinners during the Passion. The Savior is sick and suffering with love for those whom he is about to save through his sacrifice on Calvary.[85] "The voice of the soul longing with eternal love and seeking the beauty of her Maker, rings out, 'Let him kiss me with the kiss of his mouth,'" shouts fourteenth-century English mystic Richard Rolle, quoting from Song of Songs (1:2). "Until I can see my Beloved clearly," continues Rolle, "I shall sing at every remembrance of his sweet name; it is never far from mind."[86]

The idea of spiritual marriage—the mystical union of Christ with the soul—goes back to Origen's allegorical commentary on Song of Songs.[87] "When the soul has purified herself, when she burns with the fire of charity, when she shines by reason of her virtues, God takes his pleasure greatly in

---

82. Fox, *Song of Songs and Ancient Egyptian Love Songs*, 327.

83. Scheindlin, *Gazelle*, 55, 245.

84. Scheindlin, *Gazelle*, 94.

85. Jasper and Prickett, *Bible and Literature*, 188, 192. Cf. Gardner, *Book of Religious Verse*, 56-60.

86. Rolle, *Fire of Love*, 122-23. Cf. Jasper and Prickett, *Bible and Literature*, 188, 191.

87. Origen, *Song of Songs*, 21-22.

her," declares Denys the Carthusian. "He holds her familiarly like a lovely bride clasping her, caressing her, embracing her, and communicating his blessings to her abundantly."[88] The medieval Flemish mystic John Ruusbroec offers all manner of passionate metaphors: he speaks of being submerged in love; of swooning; of storms of eagerness; of embraces; of a love that burns the soul day and night; of overflowing delights; of being bruised by love. "I have become lost in his mouth," one Beguine utters, concerning Christ. Another shouts, "Oh, to drink in the glances of love and to be engulfed in them intoxicated!"[89]

Finally, John of the Cross's *Spiritual Canticle*, based on Song of Songs, is an impassioned dialogue between the Bride and Bridegroom. In his commentary, he sees the initial stanzas as displaying the purgative way—meditation and mortification; the next stanzas as the illuminative way—leading to spiritual betrothal; with later stanzas as the unitive way—culminating in marriage.[90] Listen to these various poems: "O living flame of love,/how tenderly you wound/my soul in her profoundest core!/You are no longer shy./Do it now, I ask you:/break the membrane of our sweet union."[91] "O that night of ecstasy/When the Beloved and Lover joined."[92] "My occupation: love. It's all I do."[93]

These are just some of the profound ways Song of Songs has influenced Jewish and Christian spirituality. I believe the book should be interpreted in a straightforward sense, though it can be disjointed and difficult to follow. Its elliptical style makes it appear, at times, more like a puzzle needing to be solved. That's why finding a commentator familiar with ancient Hebrew, as well as the Egyptian parallels, is so vital. The book is a profound, haunting celebration of love in all of its physical and emotional aspects. Read it, as Barth says, as a Magna Carta of the intimacy that should exist between a man and a woman.

The lovers are not fair-weather friends; they have pledged a lifelong troth. Thus, the book ends: "O Solomon, you have your multitudes

---

88. Ferguson, *Encyclopedia of Mysticism*, 174.

89. De Rougemont, *Love in the Western World*, 157–58. Cf. Wiseman, *John Ruusbroec: Spiritual Espousals*.

90. Thompson, "Spiritual Canticle," 358–59. Cf. Kavanaugh and Rodriguez, *Collected Works of St. John of the Cross*, 477.

91. Scheindlin, *Gazelle*, 39.

92. Flores, *Anthology of Spanish Poetry*, 67.

93. Flores, *Anthology of Spanish Poetry*, 71.

Introduction

of foreign wives and a large harem, but I have the one I love" (8:11–12). Edmund Spenser, that great Renaissance playwright, commemorates his own wedding in "Epithalamion," praising his wife's charms in a language reminiscent of Song of Songs:

> "Adornd with beautyes grace and vertues store,
> Her goodly eyes lyke Saphyres shining bright,
> Her forehead yvory white,
> Her cheekes lyke apples which the sun hath rudded,
> Her lips lyke cherryes charming men to byte,
> Her brest lyke to a bowle of creame uncrudded,
> Her paps lyke lyllies budded,
> Her snowie necke lyke to a marble towre,
> And all her body like a pallace fayre,
> Ascending uppe with many a stately stayre."[94]

---

94. MacLean, *Edmund Spenser's Poetry*, 438. Cf. Bainton, *What Christianity Says*, 71.

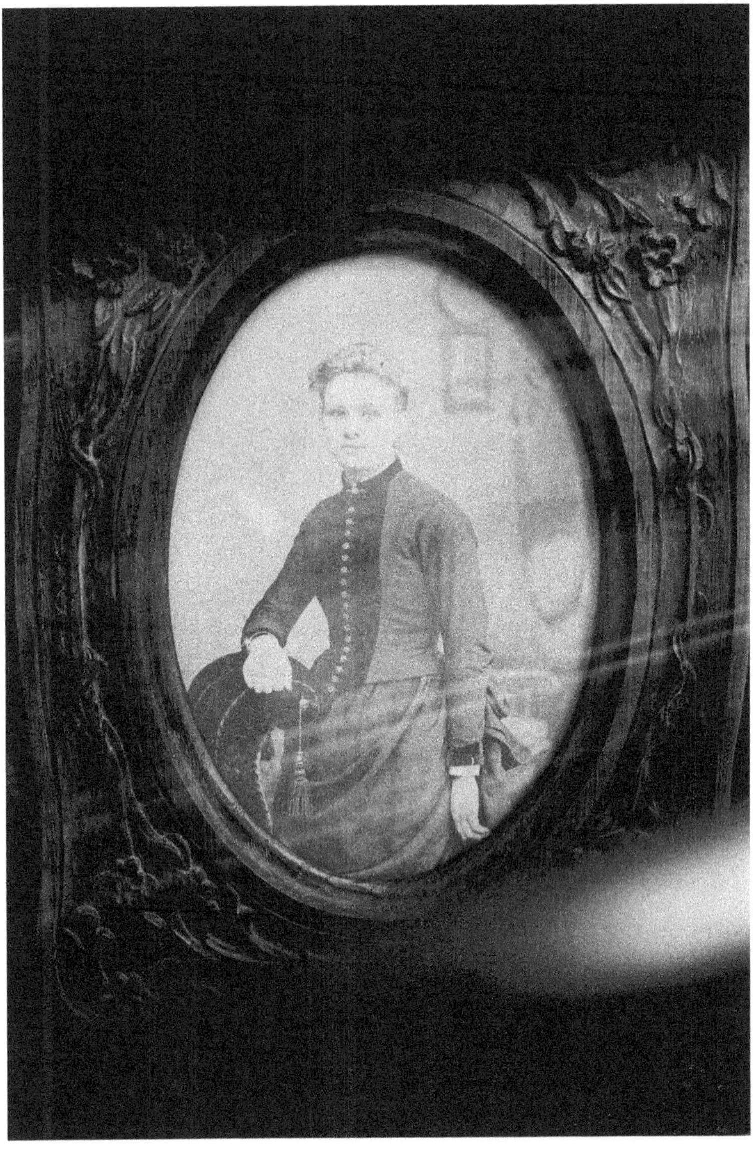

An Old, Crinkled Treasure Chest

An old, crinkled treasure chest,
I lay you on my bed,
touching your sparkling finery and dazzling jewels,
a skeleton key rattling in your lock.

No Seven Cities of Cibola,
no Nepal or kingdom of Tibet
was ever plundered more willingly
or more worth the outfitter's expense.

The quest—I must say I relished,
the dangers—imaginary, slight, and exaggerated,
the tumblers—I've jiggled,
the spoils—dispatched in a hurry.

But like a magic tinkling box,
you play soothing melodies
I love to hear, your emerald-
pewter skin glows like a twelve-tone scale.

My greed is satiated
with reproduced miniature me's,
X marks the spot,
not far from our childhood flirtations.

My advice to future buccaneers—
discard maps, smash compasses,
dig secretly and in fertile seclusion,
only five paces from your cottage door.

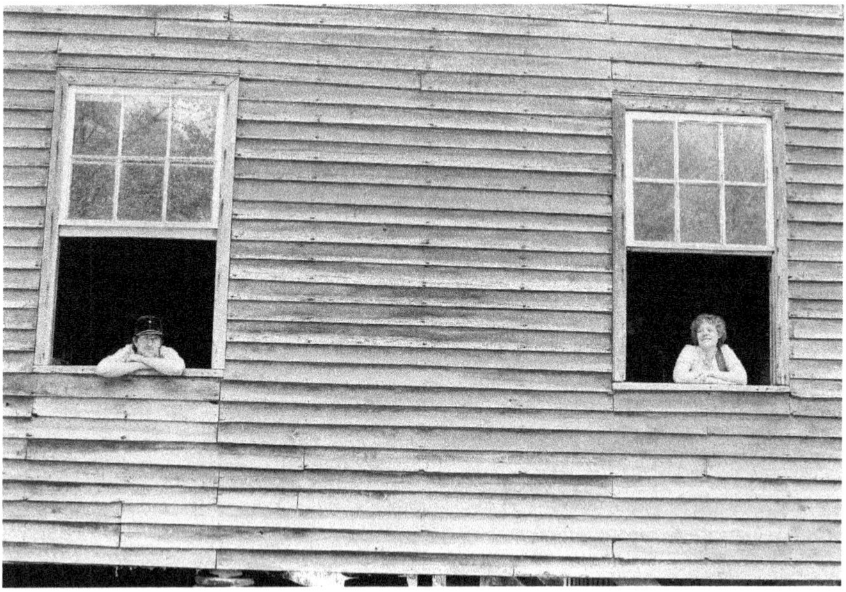

A Valentine

She loves me,
or does she not?
like the Great Mosque of Cordoba
is she white or red?
the unicorn purifies all who touch,
in a perfumed garden does it rest its head,
the black knight to the white queen.

Good-bye Pisces,
hello Aquarius,
the Lord of Nativity governs our birth,
the bridal gown is festooned
when two pink planets coincide,
the Luscher test of passion, prank-playing Holi,
will our love ripen, seeds dispersed?

Or shall April buds frost over, stunted, premature,
like a stone rippling to the pond's icy edge?
love demands Venetian blinds, far from custodial gaze,
Rembrandt's early self-portraits disturbed all,
yet who would parade him under *L'Arc de Triomphe*?
though the Serengeti plain is richest in life,
in walled Ksar love blooms.

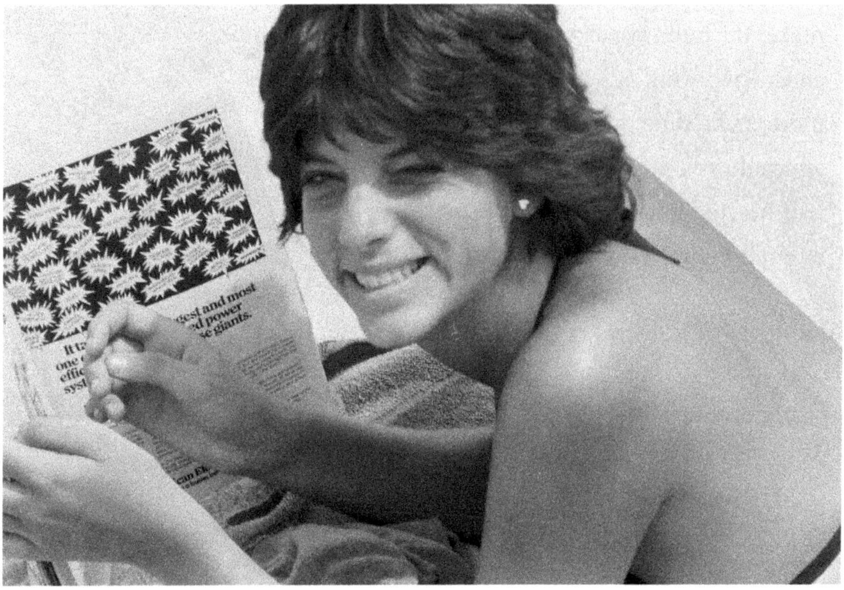
gest and most
ed power
se giants.

Love's Rags

Love's rags surpass Vanity's desires

as much as stars out-drench the moon's facade,

a hip-pocket affair

—as stealthy as a Judas priest—

outstrips the open-handed seduction

by women of the night,

a Gordian knot of bliss

makes the bull's eye arrow quiver,

an enticing wink

more enchanting than a languorous nude,

which do you prefer:

half-hearted thighs every hour

or a full-blown Barbara once a week?

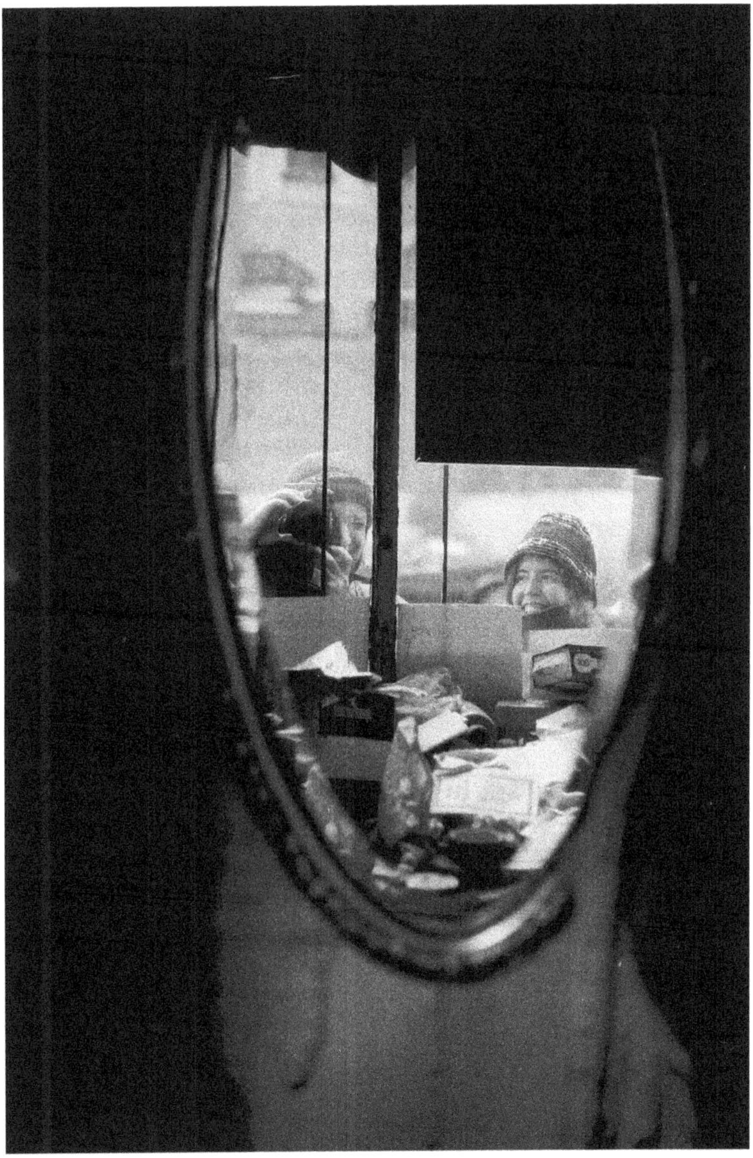

. . . how much I love you?

You ask how much I love you?
I feebly reply.
Never enough my darling
could I expound.
To what shall I compare my passions?
A dinghy ballooning in the wind.
How shall I express my longings?
As zinc admires its dipole magnet.
Your beauty—who can brush it?
Surely no Florentine or Parisian hack.
Why do I prattle on like a foolish troubadour
when I can squeeze you in my suction-cup arms?
> Your irises—bright as amber.
> Your movements graceful as a chamois' on a craggy slope.
> Your hands gentle, caressing as the incoming tide.
> Your mouth inviting as a bottlenose porpoise.

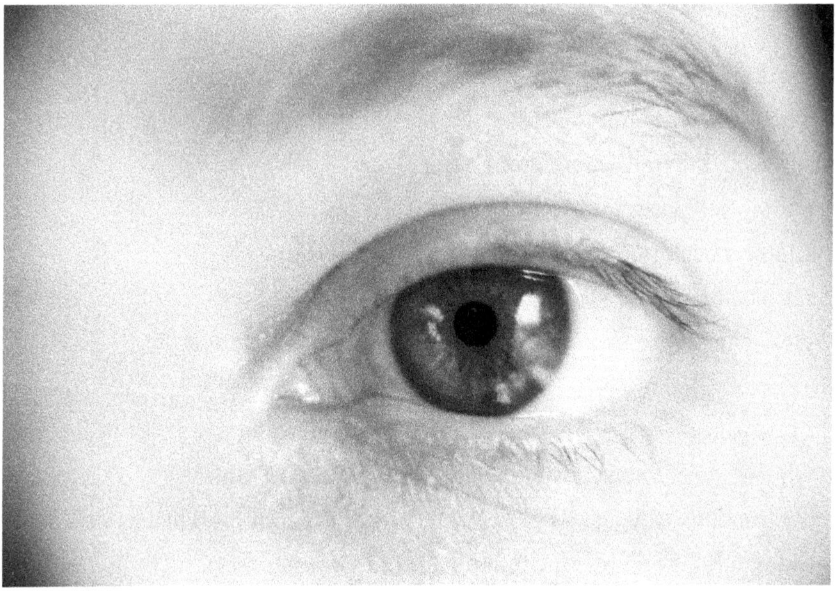

The Abduction

I kidnapped the effervescence from your eyes
and held it for ransom in the dungeon of my heart,
demanding a sealed solicitous confession
of previous indifference, stilted ingratitude,
a pledge or a signet ring of your golden turn-round,
an impecunious manifesto to an unbelieving world
that "I" indubitably, with full faculties, have been chosen by dreamy "you."

I snuck up behind you unawares during a moonlit reverie,
when your inveterate splendor was splashing about the transept and nave,
suffusing the translucent dome,
like vials of phosphorescence uncapped,
iridescence fluttering behind lattice-screen curtains,
klieg lantern arcs pulsating to luminous shadows,
glow-worms progressing through successive stages of molt.

I saw your flickering orb outside my windowsill and gasped,
laboring to confine your radiance within my chest's tomb,
yet somehow you leaked piecemeal through the shimmering crevices;
out of joint, I ordered one full millennium of penance,
called for the renewal of vows to your high carnal priest,
ordered consensual arousal and synchronized culmination,
devotion of a sort which means not so much as a wink of purgatory.

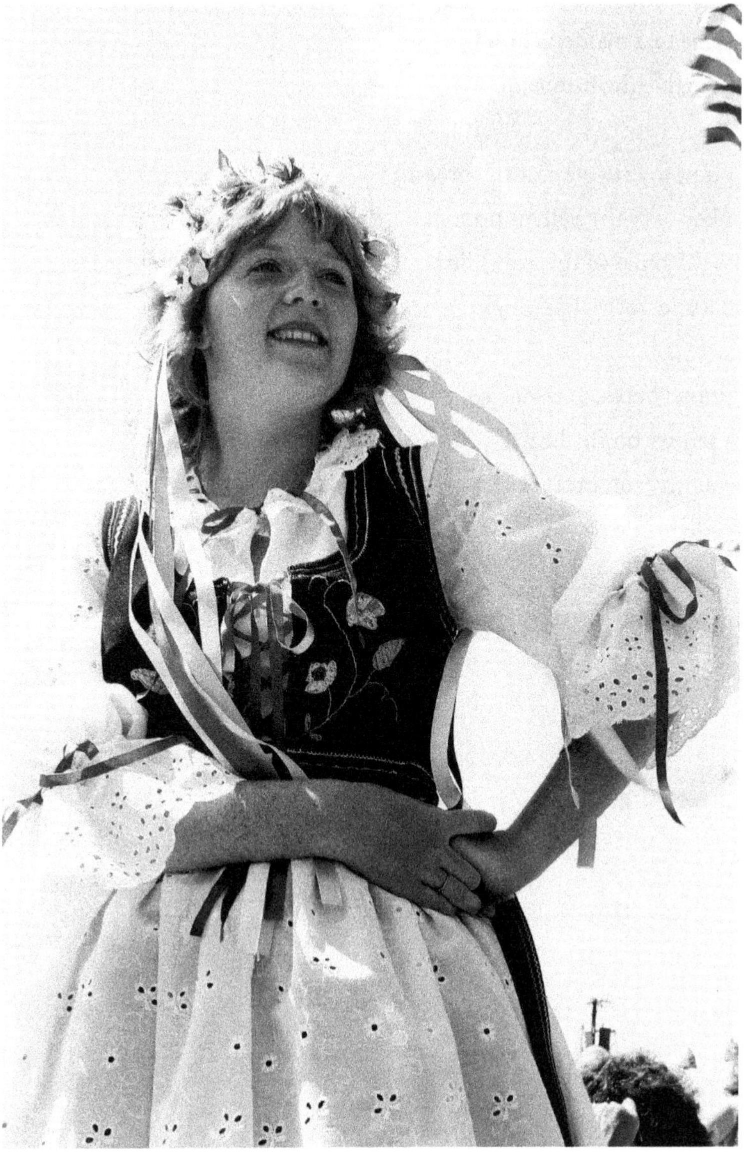

Lay Siege to a Maiden's Honor

I'll catapult thy walls,
wear down thy defenders,
lay siege to a maiden's honor,
take captive the beautiful.

I'll point my spyglass at thy breasts,
clamber over thy bellybutton,
cross the moat of thy sweet lips,
look for lucrative openings.

I'll tunnel between thy legs,
rain arrows on thy heart,
feel out thy soft buttocks,
explode inside thy secret place.

Now wilt thou signal surrender?

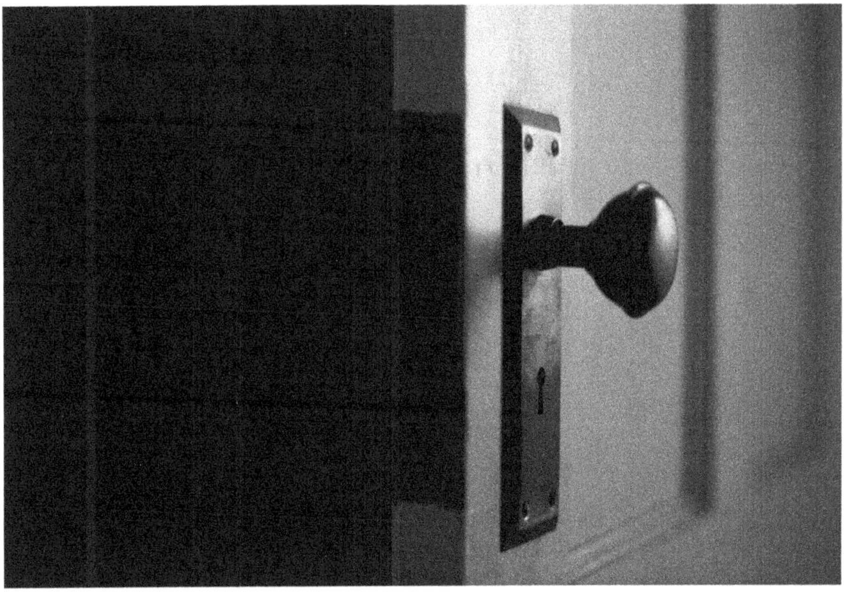

Outside Your Door

I stand at the door and knock,
will you open?
I tiptoe to your peephole,
yank on your knob and push your doorbell.

Let me slide open that glass screen,
shove your revolving turnstile,
fit my key inside your well-oiled lock,
bang hard on your gargoyle handle.

Shall I unfasten your metal latch,
pull up that iron bar,
swing open your rusty hinges,
shake all day on your Christmas bells?

I can scream myself apart like Othello,
rap coyly and softly like Mark Antony,
sigh and moan like Romeo,
connive and purr as Puss in Boots.

Why not kick the door right off its frame
like the New York Fire Department,
stand at attention like a Saint Bernard,
pick your barrels like any good professional thief?

Better to throw an epileptic tantrum,
foam and fake a heart attack,
slip through a cockroach crevice
or scrunch myself under the door like some postal dispatch.

But what do my schemes avail
if you've gone out for the night?

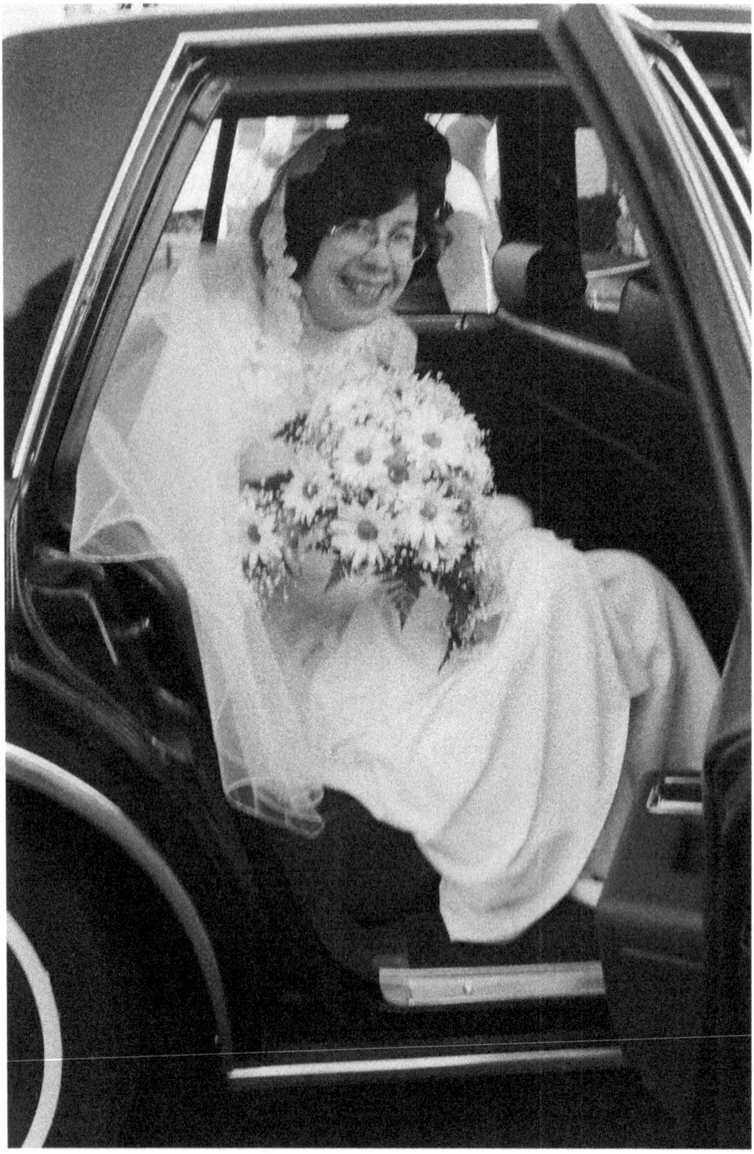

Good Juliet

Up and away my bride to be,
spontaneous giggles and chortles,
child of the Milky Way,
shyer than the tortoise
who carries its own cocoon,
born under Sagittarius not Libra,
jingling eyes, filament of honesty,
wears her soul inside out,
trusts me too completely.

Shifts her artificial horizon,
the makings of a queen,
fickle enough to scare my self-assurance,
an ornament for my elbow,
a smile to regress my rashness,
an opinion worth unfolding,
a petal spat upon by the dew, blistered
by insolent rays, torn by the selfish robin,
a heart I want more than independence,
flesh enough to scorn the casual ladies of the night,
worth a carnival of high jinx,
my faithful Juliet—and twice as amusing—

bends though never cries,
loves me like a firebird,
hangs on like putty.
I love her,
I love her
more than any suitor,
but will that suffice?

send her autographed flowers,
valentines of reckless love,
then prove my own insincerity:
demand sex.

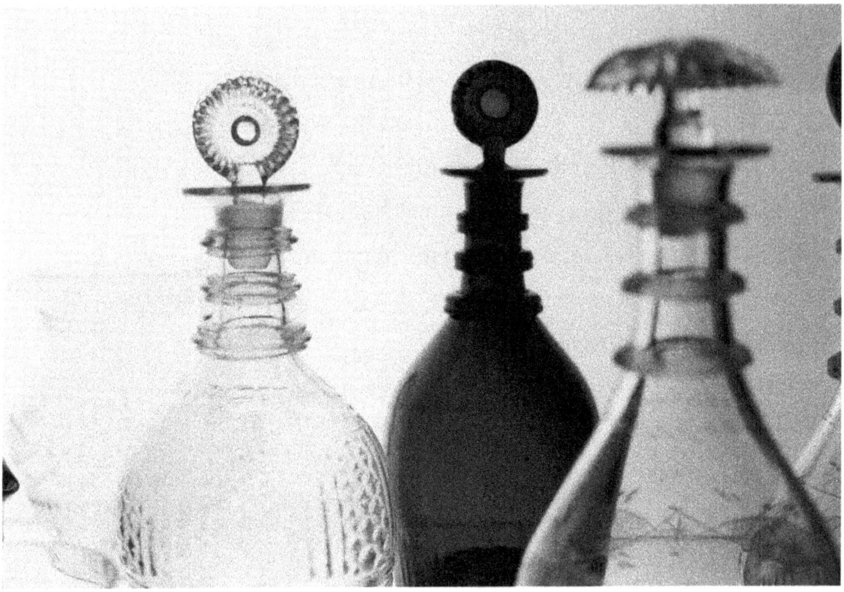

Some Loving Potion

Is there some loving potion or risqué formula
which can stir up affections in one sore disinclined,
surreptitiously arouse the genitalia
through ribald injections, succulent serums,
till professed fence sitters are stunned,
stony walls o'erleaped,
imagined whispers and sighs
suffuse and brighten the room,
with the desired one lying nude, vivid on your pillow.

Can the object of your affections change color,
susceptible to a sorcerer's wand or an alchemist's stone,
so one's helpmeet is chosen by a chemical matchmaker?
Or are life's charms so discreet,
they needs must thump the heart,
not simply whet the sweet and sour papillae of the tongue?
Happiness resides then not in a pill
nor bliss in a cold, Colchis kiss,
as even Medea's fabled arts couldn't hold Jason's ambitions in check.

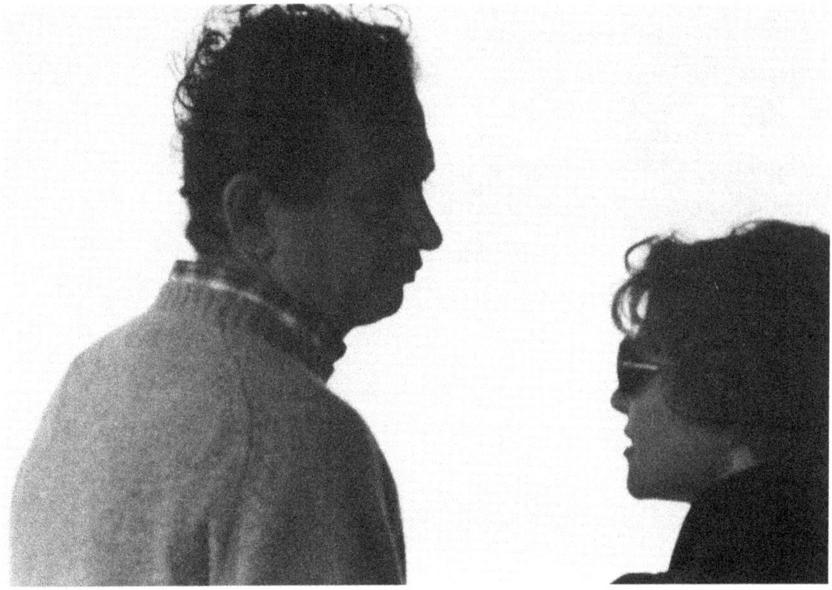

Determined Lovers

Melancholy lovers parted wet
on foolhardy ridge,
the bonds of triumphant death to them seemed stronger
than the strain memory of separate existence.

Love laughs at deadbolts, fences,
disapproving glances,
forbidden rendezvous,
threats of annihilation.

Though it be the king's decree
that races intermingle not,
feuding clans of Hatfields and McCoys
might still enjoy surreptitious favors.

Castrated Abelard may
hold and satisfy paramour Heloise
in Platonic spheres,
Pyramus and Thisbe unite beyond the grave.

Walls have never stopped invaders
nor determined lovers for long,
—just increased the time spent
in decoy maneuvers and obverse stratagems.

How many forms did Zeus contrive
to deceive jealous Hera?
> pyrite shower,
> tender, lowing bull,
> elegant, high-necked swan,
> whiskered satyr,
> antic, changeable cloud.

And if you think these aren't enough,
what of the devices of Apollo
against willful, disinterested Daphne?
Why, he would peel the bark right off her trunk.

But Hymen's scale can be bought
with relatively minor self-sacrifice,
so why choose otherworldly meeting places
where only souls are nude?

Earth is meant for marrying,
the enraptured bee sings in her nectar
in all 64 positions,
here two learn to transcend the heavy, sluggish, sublunar soil.

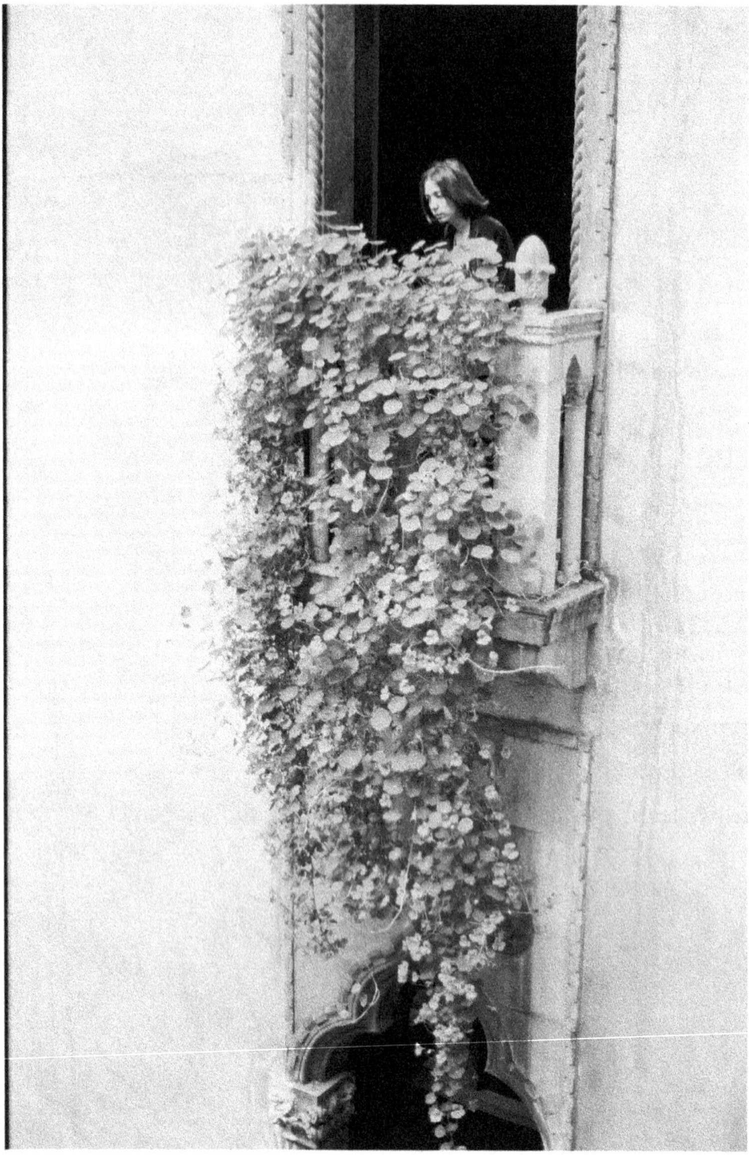

The Song of the Young Brave

I love the way she smiles—
like one of those Olmec jars
during intercourse—
agitated, soft, and wild,
which speaks of happiness and need.

I long to enclose my skin in hers,
fortify our Walnut Canyon cliff dwelling,
climb ladders up and down her breasts,
painted marauders we won't fear,
we've land and water and sky.

Baskets to weave, blankets to embroider, inlaid silver necklaces—
she'll raise our papoose,
simmer our roots, herbs, and maize,
I'll hunt jackrabbit and deer,
war councils will be unknown.

Let redoubtable adventurers set forth,
stargazers build high their observatories,
architects draw blueprints for adobe villages,
we two will lie content
with earthenware smiles.

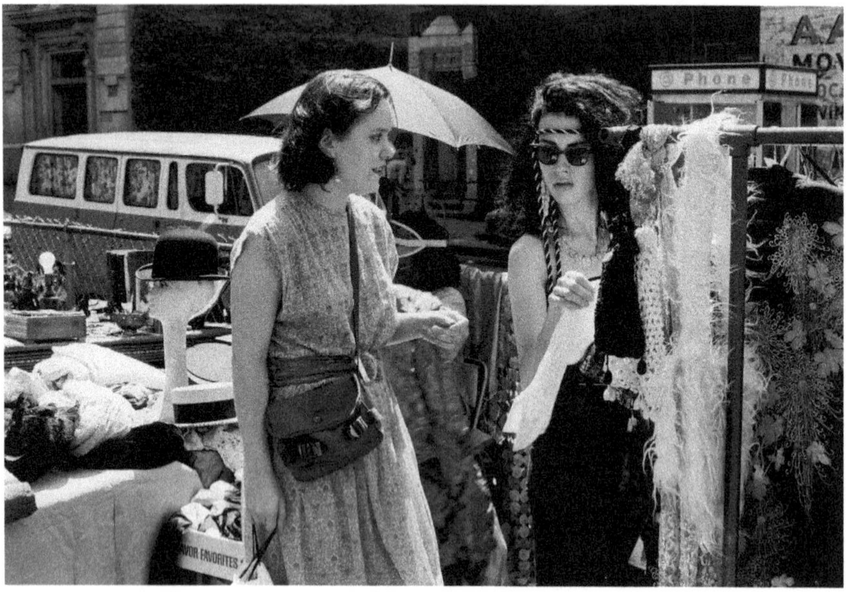
Phone
Phone

To Please My Friend

To please my friend,
I'll put on this garish hat and horrid gown,
make-believe that I'm a fairy princess,
who can turn this wayside cottage into a rococo palace
for lacquered carriages to promenade by,
conveying powdered, bespectacled courtiers;
Melissa will swoon before some enamored gallant
who foolhardily vows to perform a string of staggering feats
to win her matchless hand.

Then I'll smear on exotic rouge and civet perfume,
so as to infatuate a queue of suitors
till our friendship is stretched and strained,
fomenting intrigues and counteraccusations,
while I coyly strut behind my silk eyelet fan;
just when the mutineers are about to uncap a truth-telling phial,
I'll confess, blurt out my blackened plans
to some lecherous Dominican friar,
who will soon be at a loss over which of us to renounce his vows.

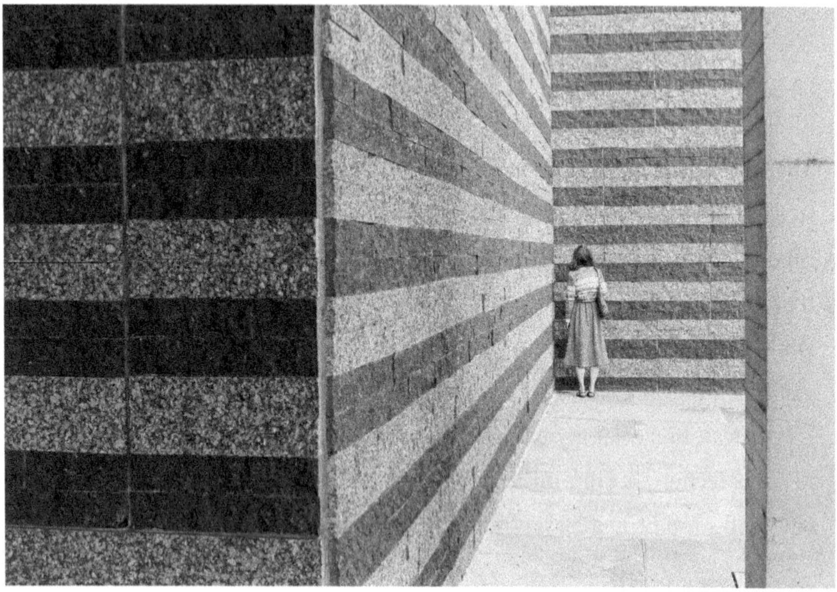

After a Hell-Raising

After a hell-raising, there's a considerable lull,
when both parties regroup,
conscience-stricken over their excesses,
words can never say enough,
there's a hush in the summer air
as after an electrical discharge,
faces are wet, concealed,
eyes wounded, withdrawn,
so we reach for that not yet visible hand
which can set the world right,
the reconciling encounter
neither side is eager to commence,
so couples, municipalities, provinces,
swing, collide, and, on occasion, conjoin.

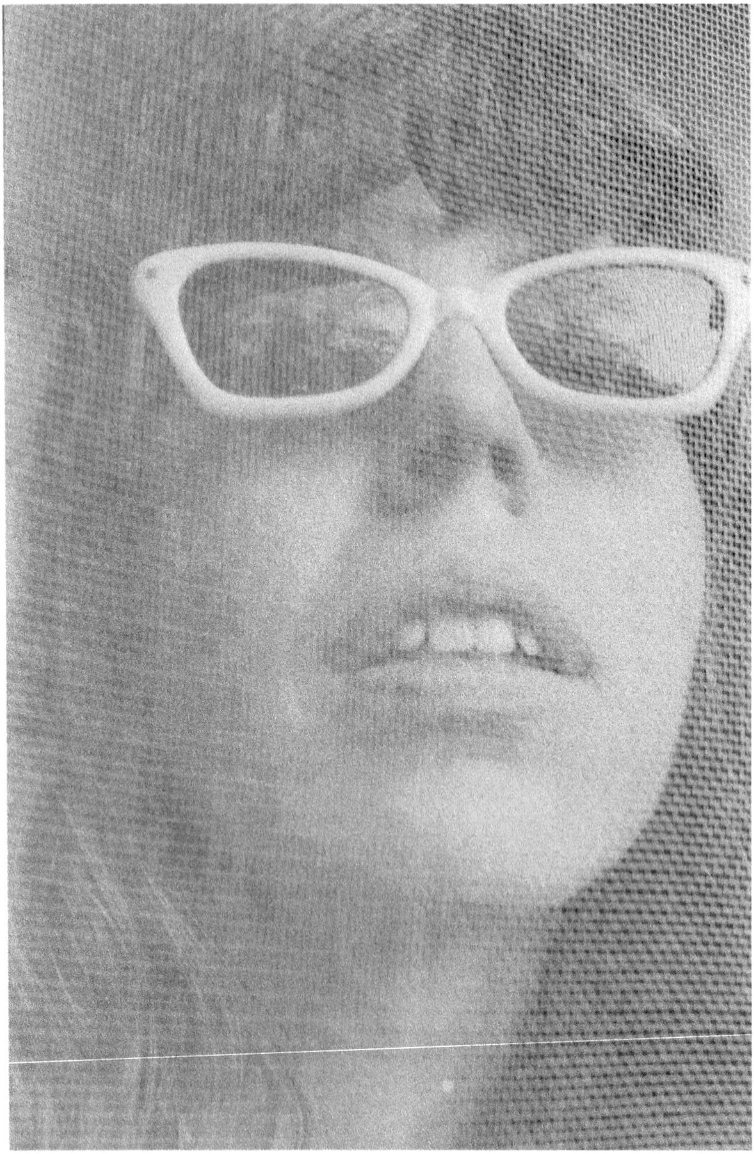

Critical Likeness

In the reflecting pool of your two eyes
I see my own shimmering imperfections.

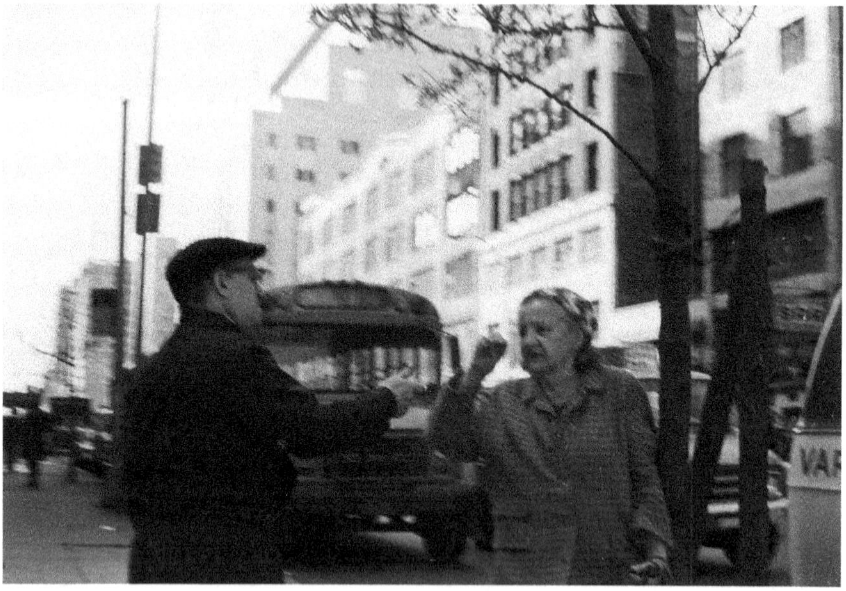

Why Don't You Listen?

Why don't you listen when I speak—
cotton swabs blocking hammer, anvil, and stirrup,
perceptual filters screening out undesired frequencies,
wax accumulating outside the drum
or hearing aid turned down far too low?

You blankety-blank—afraid to hear the truth,
you so-and-so, can't stand criticism,
or does my vehemence ring hollow,
betray my own vacillation?

No, it's just the male ego threatened,
win every argument by voice vote
or slug my way to the finish line,
men marry women they can dominate.

Two split asunder by chain-reaction squabbles,
both sides too resolute to yield,
send in an arbitration panel or trained mediators
to restore the detached auditory nerve.

Words deflected, bounce off into space
or somehow become garbled in the first 20 feet,
dialogue delayed by "I've heard it all before,"
minds embrace counter-productive reconciliation.

Three hundred ohms from one auricle to the next—
splice the wires or put in copper strands,
divergences are preordained for this crucible of faith,
GOD your neighbor is the decisive litmus test.

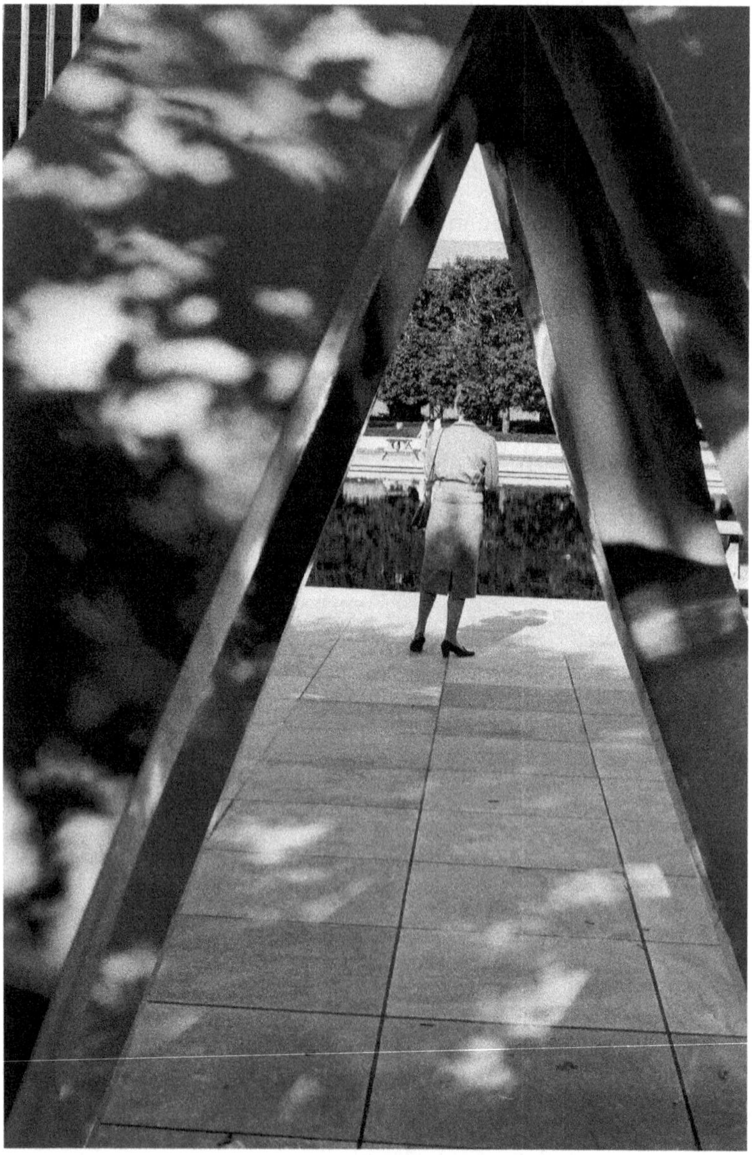

Go Away and Nest Elsewhere?

Go away and nest elsewhere?
First, tell kumquats to go to seed.
Berate the sow to butcher her squealing pig
Or badger the sun to poke out its offending eye.
Like the interstellar vacuum my brain would collapse a pea,
Or like the *Hindenburg* dirigible my heart would disappear,
My anima set adrift in an off-white, waterless sea.
Hold me then till dawn raise her unseemly lid.
'Twere safer abed in Sodom than your false lover's chest;
His gifts are treacherous shoals to ground a cabin cruiser,
His arms, tentacles to paralyze a gem,
His promises more hollow than the chocolate-covered rabbit.
For six years I've gleaned your fertile ground,
Lie fallow now one in seven—'tis your jubilee,
(Or soil your matron loveliness on that braggart clown).

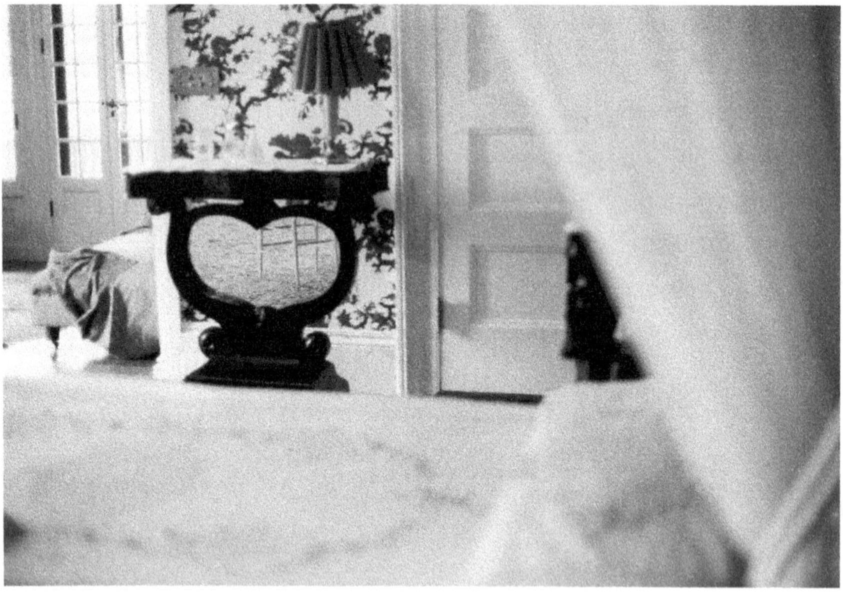

Last Night

I crept into your bed last night;
the wind howled so loud,
your arms seemed so strong,
I kissed your chest and stomach.
You put your hand below my waist.
We parted (Alcestis and Admetus)
—what fears? I forgot.

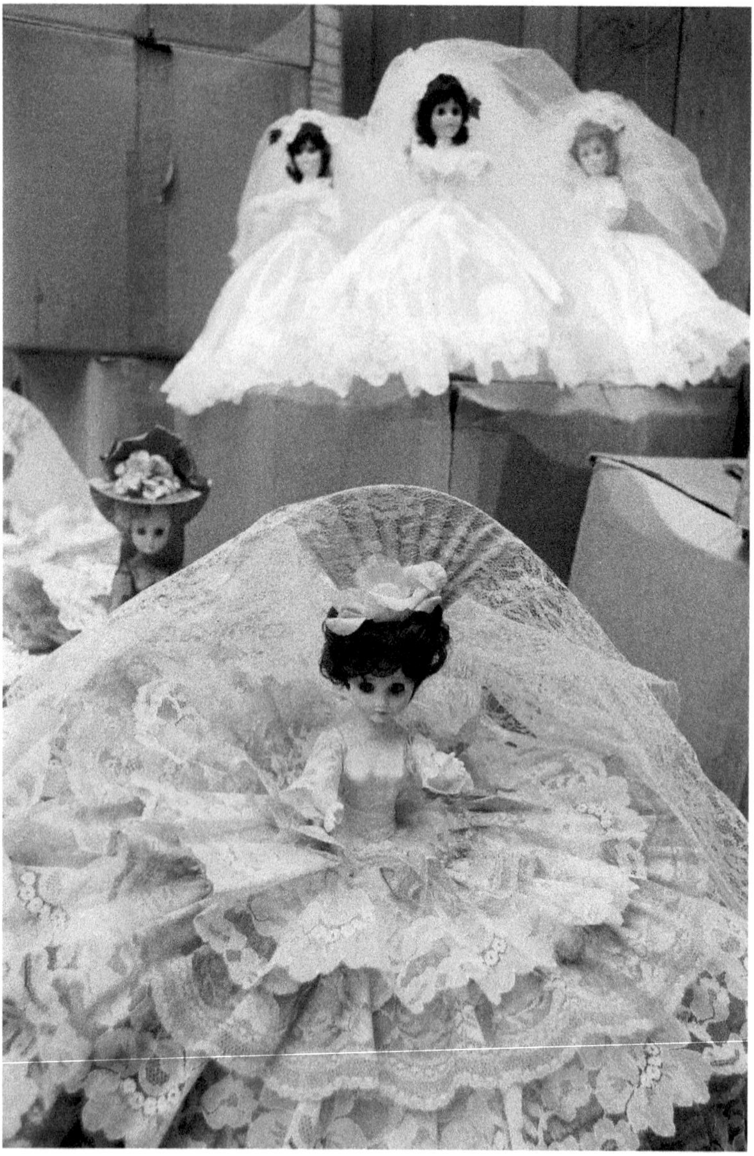

Of a St. Agnes' Night

Stick a pin in your sleeve,
recite the *Pater Noster*,
and you'll dream of the one you'll marry
of a St. Agnes' Night.

God help you if he's comely and bright,
wears a Brooks Brothers suit and suede shoes,
drives a long black Mercedes,
he'll become an insider in the stock exchange
and you'll own a vast estate along the Hudson—
till the next time the market panics.

Or should he show a flair for sports,
do the hat trick with his tennis racket
or the alley-oop in hoops,
you'll be as merry as DiMaggio
as long as the hot streak lasts,
but how will you react when he's a has-been, retires at forty-one?

Maybe your vision will clear
and you'll elope with a swaggering soldier,
his regiment will travel to exotic climes,
establish stuttering camaraderie with umpteen nationalities,
yet when war breaks out,
you'll wring your eyes on your children's shoulders.

Of, if you sleep under the wrong herb,
you may end up with a scarecrow of a poet,
who is immersed in literary arcana, each day
he'll hang out rough drafts for the birds to peck—
watch for his violent mood swings—
my advice, blot him out and dream again.

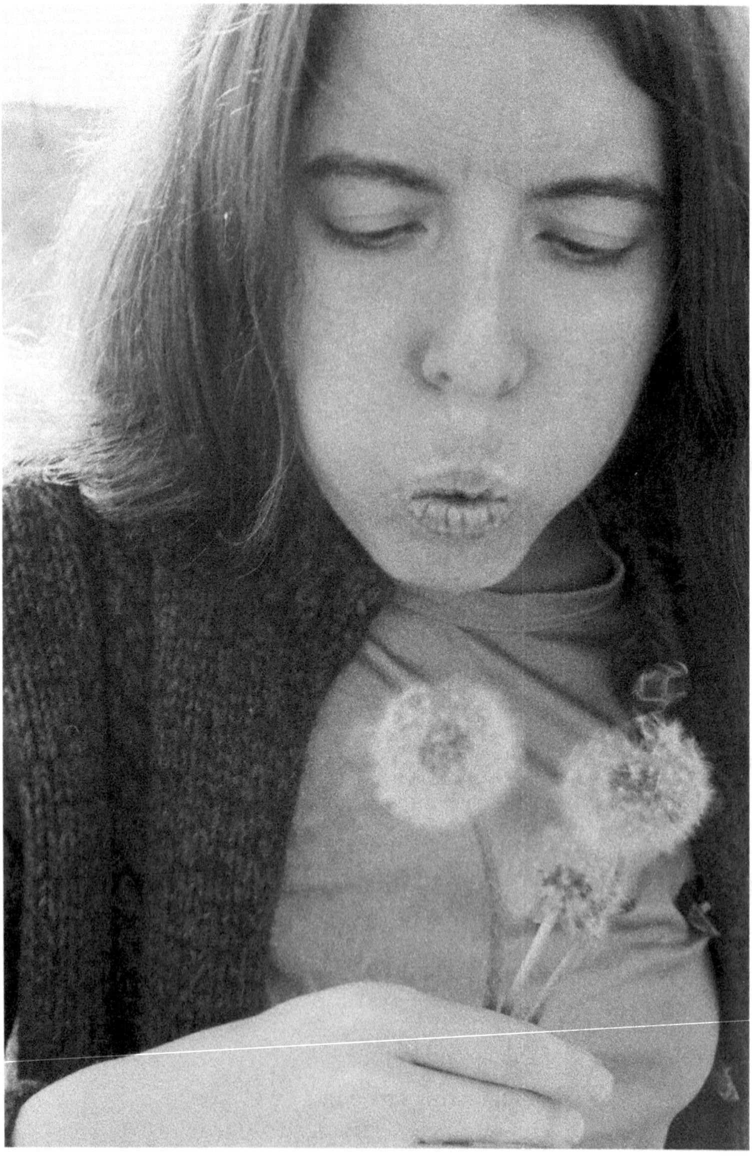

Scamper Away Now, Phoebus

Scamper away now, Phoebus,
eclipse your dying photons
for this nocturnal rite,
a maiden's virtue I'll be venting—
quite within my rights—
a head I'll pierce in imitation Eden,
like an octopus I'll constrict my blessed prey.

You be the pistil, I'll be the stamen,
cross-fertilize the onion and the clover,
ply the weft with a fertile needle,
form an intimate bond to commit a lascivious act,
the projectile ringing through the loop
wins a pubescent favor.

Interlocking two-in-one, a fleshly horizontal plane,
is this the fruit God said you shall not eat?
heretics have oft entertained the doctrine
with no support from Paul,
sex and love, a mystery unraveled,
marriages are certified in heaven, annulled in a court of law.

Put a little extra on your sinkerball,
grease the fingers with something sweet,
turn on the reverberator, hang on tight,
shoot the rapids, nestle into a whirlpool,
connect on the old Statue of Liberty play.

When the doldrums come, and come they must,
remove not the prophylactic because of some pope's admonition,

successive children in a troubled world may overpopulate a couple's mind,
raise the misery index up to nine
—even sacred injunctions can be misconstrued.

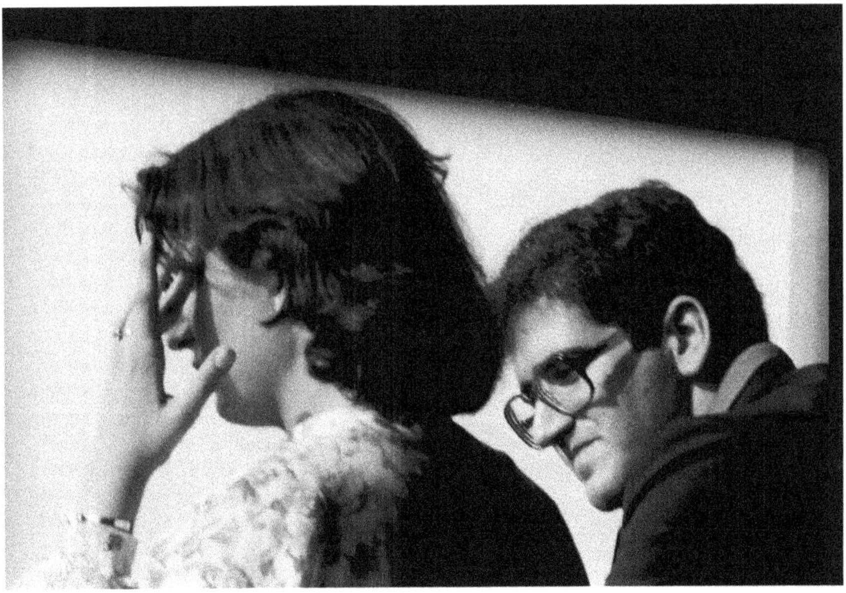

Either This or That

Either this or that,
dog for cat,
green peppers in place of mushrooms,
a lira for a pfennig,
a chicken or turkey sandwich,
a vault versus a crematorium,
a cane instead of a walker,
nonfat dry milk *oder* dehydrated vanilla,
bankers accept surrogates
as long as it's always gold.

My love is more than adequate
now that you're degenerate bronze,
I'll exchange our nuptial writ
for a Lilliputian box of snuff,
our rum and sherry wedding cake
for a nitroglycerine pill,
the bands we proffered earnestly
for plutonium rods of *amor*,
the dowry your stingy father gave
for a hackneyed stay-at-home.

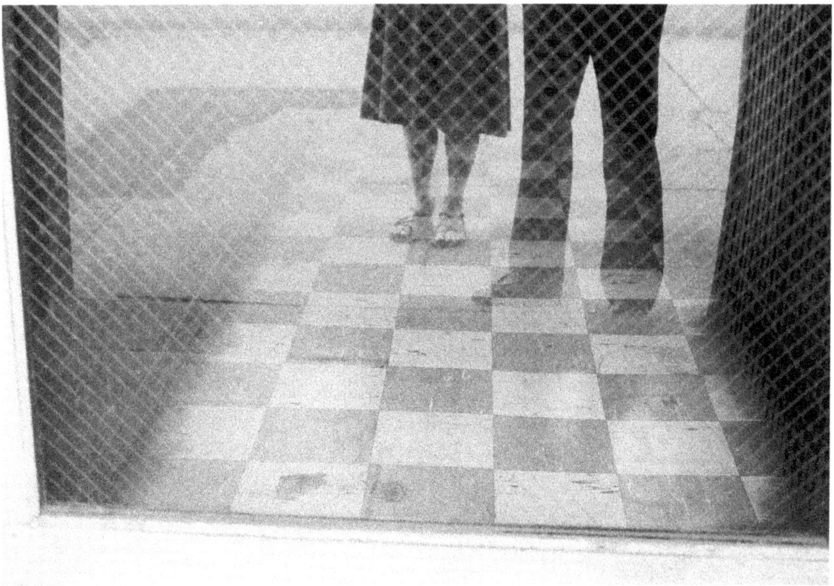

The Wind Has Turned

The wind has turned,
so my heart is bitter cold,
once you fairy-tapped outside my ledge,
tinkled your ankle bells, and I flew
to Oz, what we mistook for troth
was only our mating rhythm.

In your alluring garden
petals closed, pods burst, your sticky
nectar caressed my groins,
I felt drained like a sugar maple,
bleary red my eyes,
reposed and slumbering upon your lap.

Beauty ebbs and flows,
despair like spring kicks all else out,
doubt and trust swell like the churning sea,
we tried, but self-adoration
prevented our intermingling,
like egg-yolk tempera that will not set.

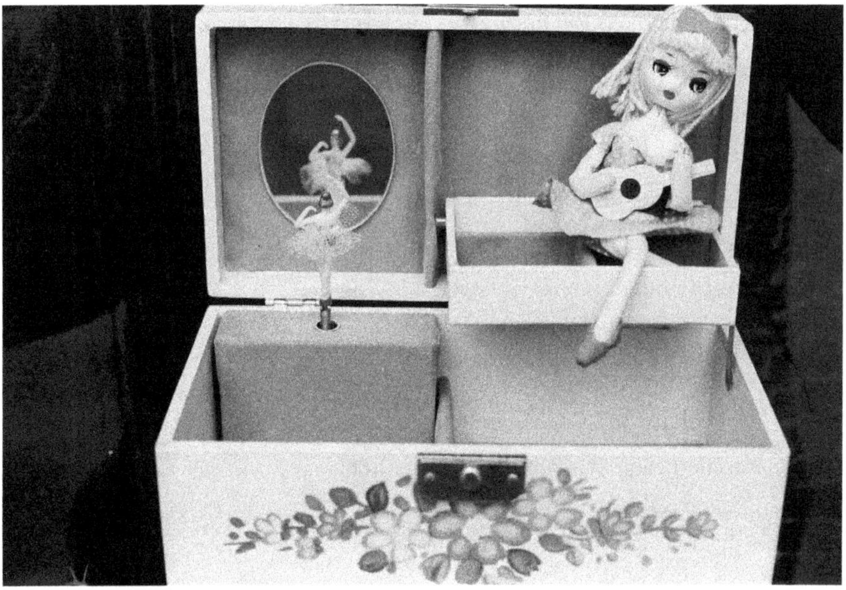

The Music Box

The music box goes round and round
and I hear a winsome melody
which mesmerizes me like soothing kisses
—my soul felt fluid in your muscular hands.

We used to hum the bars in unison
when anger threatened to overthrow our vows,
when relatives poked too hard at tender wounds,
when one of us inadvertently loosed the strands which made us strong.

I recall you whistling the chorus on our 25th,
us waltzing across the floor at 3/4 time,
I, your petal, was wrapped inside your sepal arms,
then lay resplendent before my nectar-loving bee.

I sang alto,
you bellowed out bass (usually off-key),
we made such exquisite percussion together,
our audience swelled, then subsided.

Gradually, though, you developed a minor, melancholy plaint,
it grew so raucous, discordant,
I wanted to have you tuned,
but I didn't know where or how.

Then one evening you gritted your teeth
and refused to join in,
I knew you had taken up some new sound
and didn't need my weird harmonic.

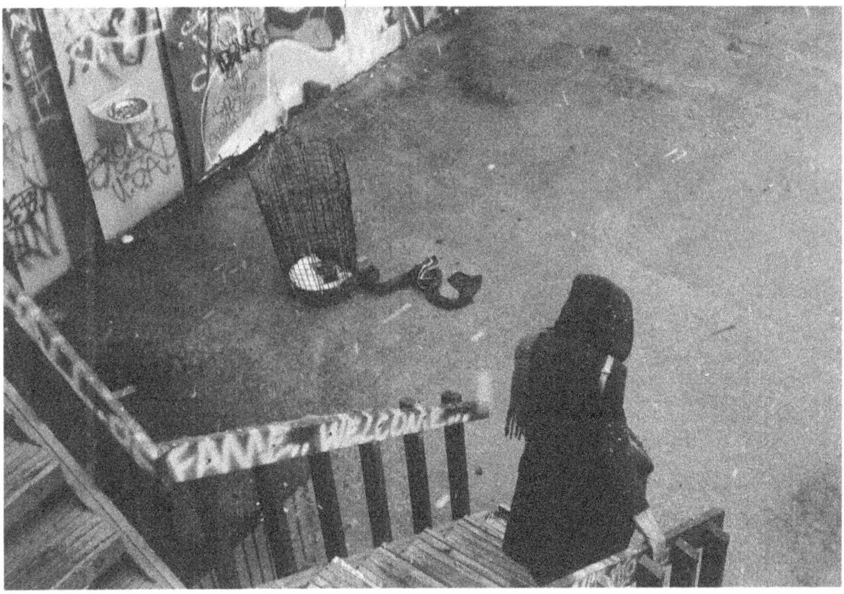
FAME.. WELCOME..

M

A teasing echo
slanting down the corridor of years,
a faint, receding taper
that emblazons the world of the imagination
like Dante's Beatrice or Petrarch's Laura,
when I encounter her now
it's in mesmerizing angles,
fragments of impossibility
like the alibis biographers invent.

If I had been less awkward, less naive,
could our arcing lines have touched,
intertwined around the streamered Maypole,
consummated in wedding bells and vows?
Sometimes I linger among Pluto's shades,
make love to idealized ghosts,
for the mind is not content with the present,
it likes to revise old maps, dig up
buried treasure from cobwebbed, planked-over floors.

I thought I loved you,
that wasn't so cruel,
but inattention and foolish banter
drove in lovelorn, careless wounds.
How fortunate to be a child bride
or marry your first sweetheart—
when the bandages still hold.
Later the gashes bleed forever,
neither cauterize nor clot.

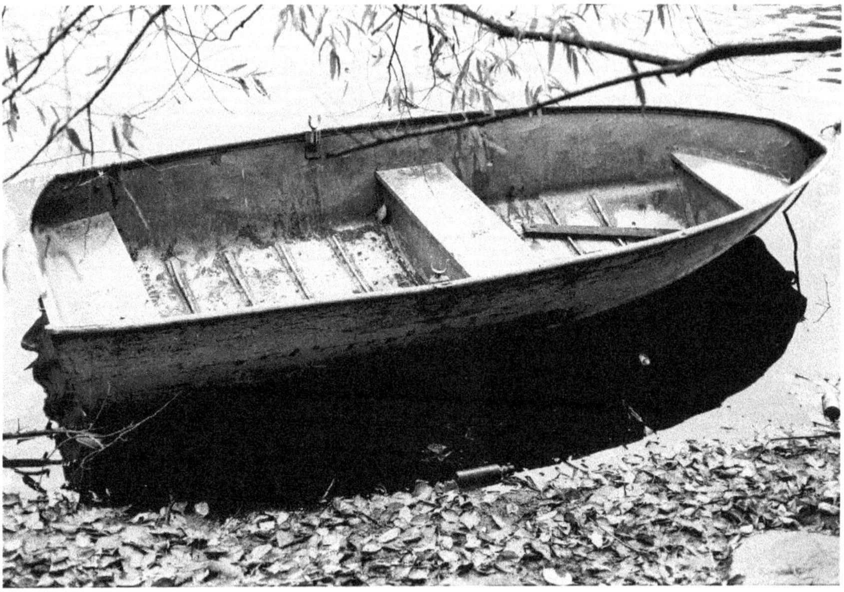

Tears Are Outlawed

'Tis a revolution since last we met,
when beggarly autumn clamped us together
for one elated afternoon, to reminisce
and prattle on like old lovers will,
to flatter your girlish fancy,
mew like adolescent Persians must.

Under the sprawling chestnut we snatched
at one another's sighs, sucked on red raspberries
or slurped our chocolate malts, unchaperoned
we fox-trotted round the pond, rowed and
rowed past dusk's semaphore,
counted stars much like empyrean gems.

That was before Cinderella's slipper
shrunk, Prince Charming flicked into a
frog, you bounded off for Oberlin
and I enlisted, our feathery habitation
evaporated when my helicopter knees
were cut off.

Sure, tears are outlawed
in this game we invented light years ago,
only tranquil dreams are e'er acknowledged
till death boots in our door,
but this once—let us redeem
our old misgivings, co-mingle our guilt with our joy.

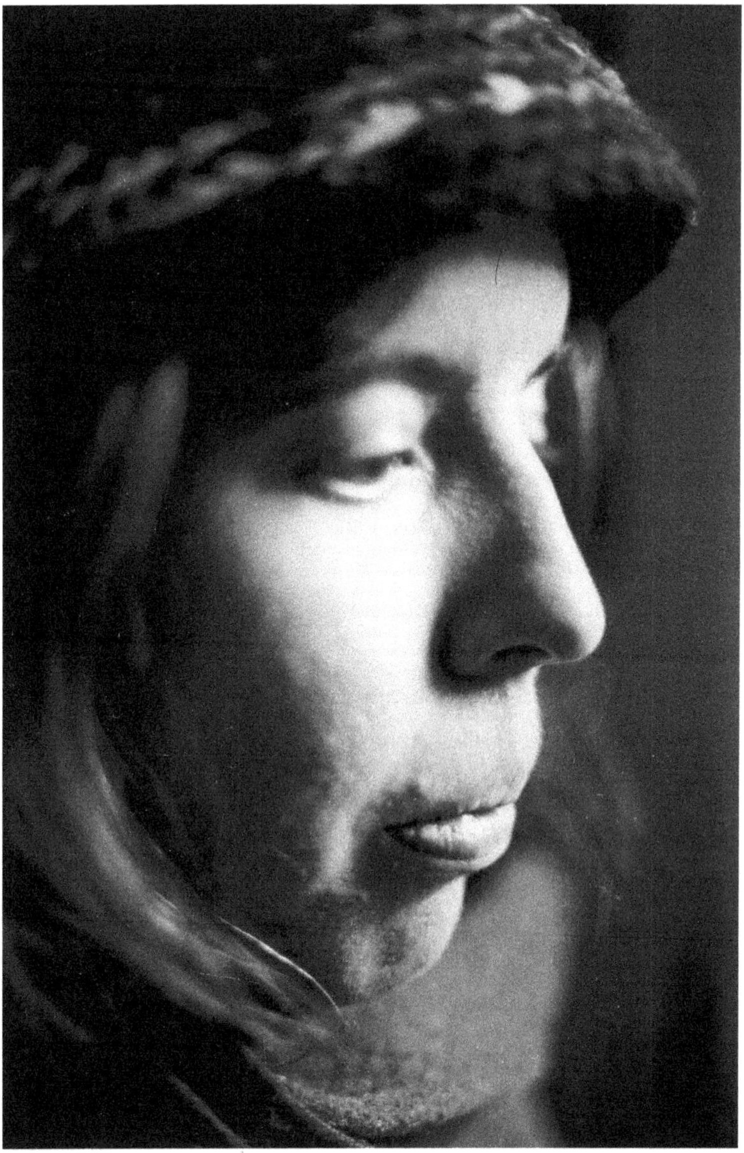

The Imprint of Love

an obsequious sigh,
a lovelorn fetal image,
a carbon copy kiss,
a frozen reflection of levity,
a smoked glass similitude,
a porous plastic bust,
a Velazquez mirror labyrinth,
duplicate aberration,
a dodged and cropped translucent pin-up,
a hybrid, dwarf, or muted twin,
a doppelgänger hug
identical to its original,
a faithless reproduction or outright parody,
a forged signet or flawed iridescent ring,
a lover's concoction without the recipe,
an inferior or cut-rate imitative orgasm
(copy-cat coitus),
a toy miniature or overblown courting ritual,
a Japanese import, a silk screen chiaroscuro,
a postcard-sized valentine,
the portrait of duplicity,
a template or *Kama Sutra* etching,
a screened, primary hue silhouette,
a matted shadow,
a gold leaf snapshot or folio edition,
convex above the *primum mobile*,
concave below,
a needlepoint romance,
a mirage of lust with a hallucinogenic supplement,
a polished silver, quartz, or diamond ruse,
a klieg light or magic lantern tragedy.

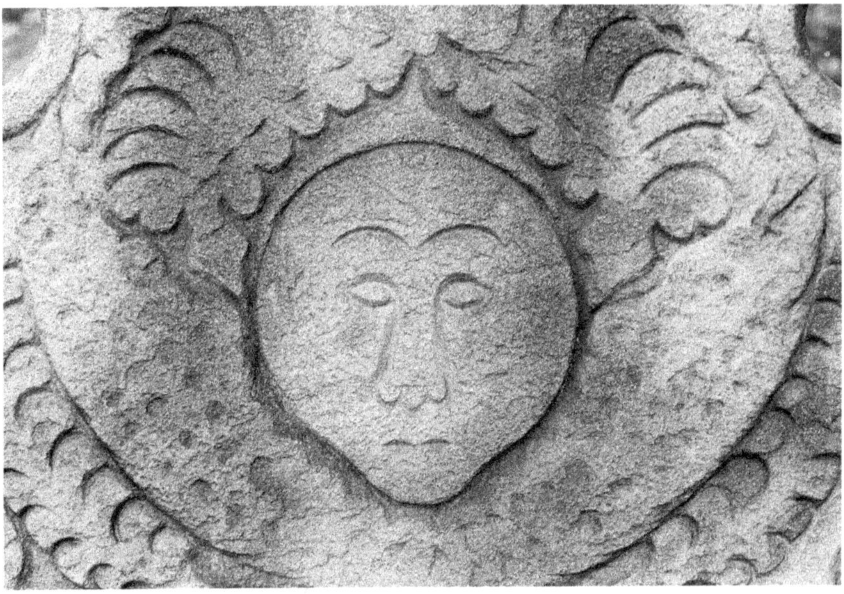

The Keepsake

The necklace you wore
I gave to you three New Years ago,
part alloy, part pure;
it came to symbolize our metallic passions
like a jade disk which welcomes Heaven.

The swelling mushroom entered the vermilion gate,
like Su Song's puppet tower
we rang the hours together,
our sympathies dovetailed so sweetly—
oracle bones split in half,
dragonflies fleeing before the storm.

I finger the yellow loops
of those gleaming trinkets you received,
a fourth sits wrapped up in your drawer,
I wanted so to impress you dear
with golden brooches and tinkling promises,
but here, let them commemorate this slab of stone.

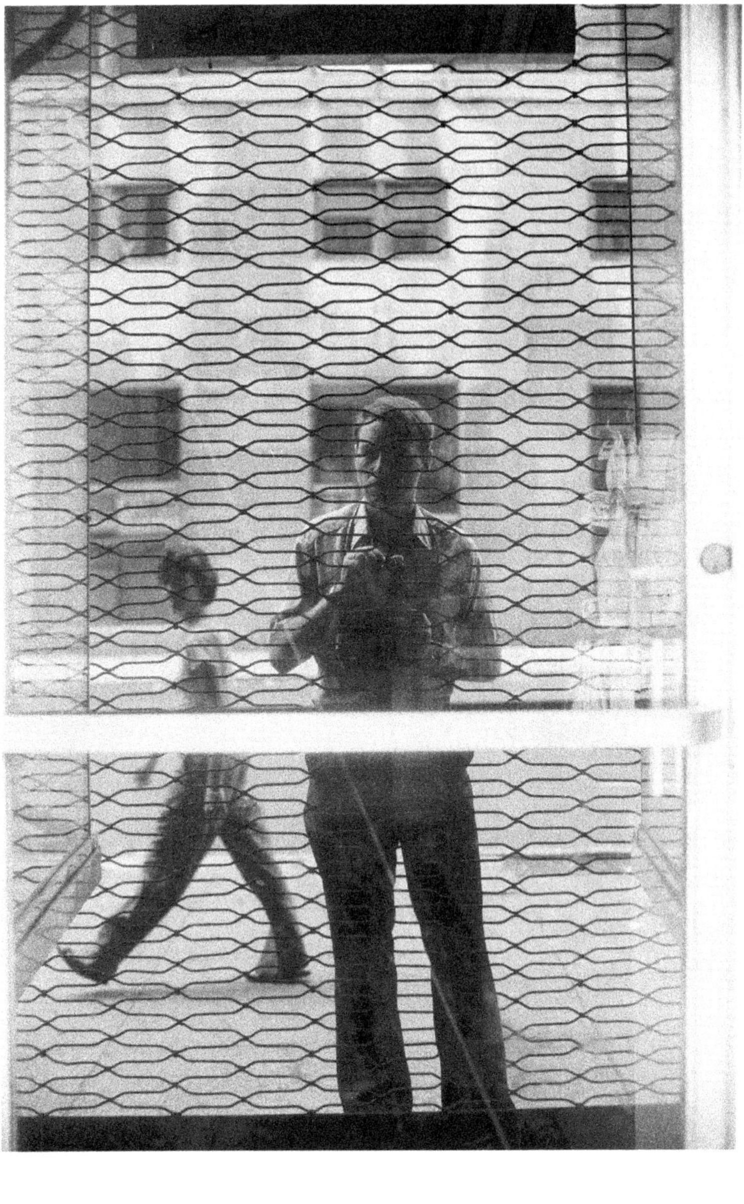

A 25-Year-Old Menopause Man

There's a paper heart on the mantel,
a faded carnation in the blue lapel,
two half-opened letters near my Victrola,
it's February 14th—and Cupid's quiver is barren.

Will Orpheus never strum his lyre?
are these tattered keepsakes forever to be mine?
can't Aphrodite coax the lovely facade?
is my bunk still one depression deep?

Foreplay without culmination,
courtship but never the ring,
secret desires that just don't materialize,
a 25-year-old menopause man.

The yin and the yang at opposite ends of the spectrum,
Eros grudgingly celibate,
a Platonic cerebral union,
the germ of life wantonly strangled.

Alone and unhappy,
a self-mutilated solitaire,
missed my election,
now glumly wait for decay.

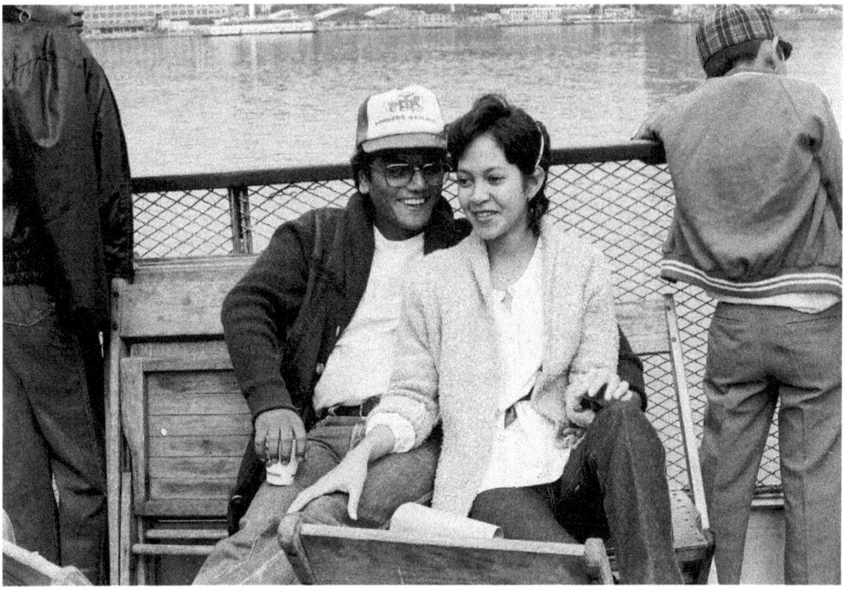

My Flaming Meteor

Punctual as a star
came my flaming meteor,
he brightened my translucent atmosphere
with homemade tunes and silly, self-conscious jokes,
while studying my sensuous, inviting contours,
he, for a time, refrained from complementing
those panting gaps with masculine-erect intrusions,
holding me in a strong, warm, sheltering light,
soon, though, he planted oval garlands on my green-fresh lips,
crushed my bare to his hairy chest,
for hours we perched like cooing birds
shuttling between enraptured flowers,
our bodies entwined into one seamless whole
as Tristan and Iseult or the dreams of Layla and Majnun,
soon a chirping third fluttered about our nest,
how strange that Proust-like associations linger on,
breathless, heart-shaped as the night sky
where they first shone.

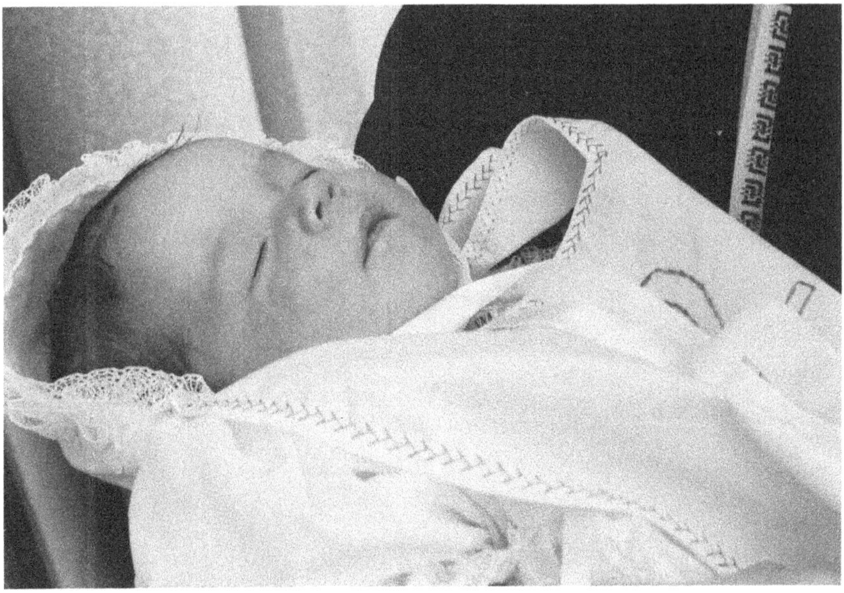

How Do They Come?

Ful oft paet gegoneo, mid godes meahtum
("Thanks be to God, two becomes three.")
—"The Fortunes of Men"[1]

How do they come,
those cherubs who replenish the earth—
still with the tinsel of innocence
or wholly forged in iniquity?

When the umbilical cord is pulled away,
do they suffer a shock that jars lifelong?
when the womb dissolves their liquid envelope,
does the half-fish become a mammal?

What does he feel under glass
with gloves and germs on the attack?
is he armed with a resourceful cranium?
will he instinctively burp and vomit up his foes?

If he still can't reason or believe,
how can pouring water make him clean?
is his godfather a screen for *tabula rasa*?
or will evil slip through any human sieve?

And why does he weep for no apparent reason?
is he depressed, or are his diapers wet?
of course, he wants milk and love, but will that suffice
for that sleeping Sphinx that has no riddle?

---

1. Delanty and Matto, *Word Exchange*, 283.

What! Does he cling with violence to his mother's breast,
forsake his father and snub his peers?
now who'll remind him of his obligation
to wean the human race from contaminated bottles?

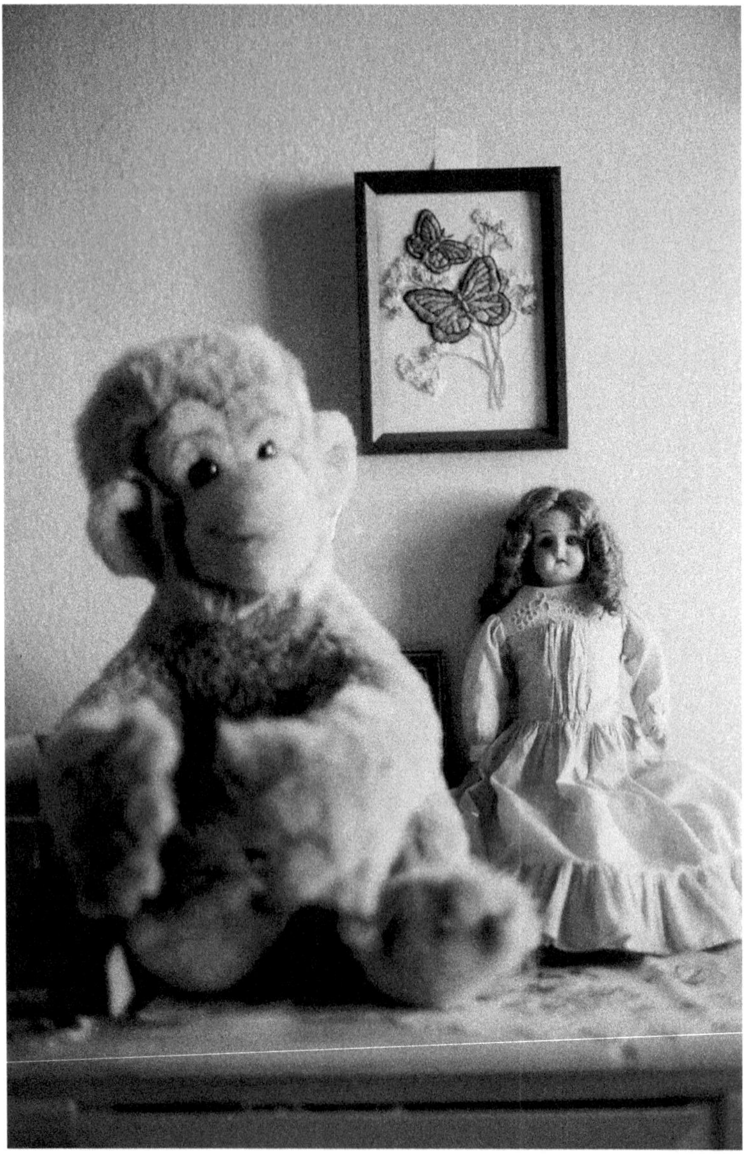

Baby's Playpen

Origami tigers, soft, molded elephants,
mechanical barking dogs,
tweed cobras that can be picked up and squeezed,
plastic pacifiers, nipples which suck air.
No wonder his whole body yawns.

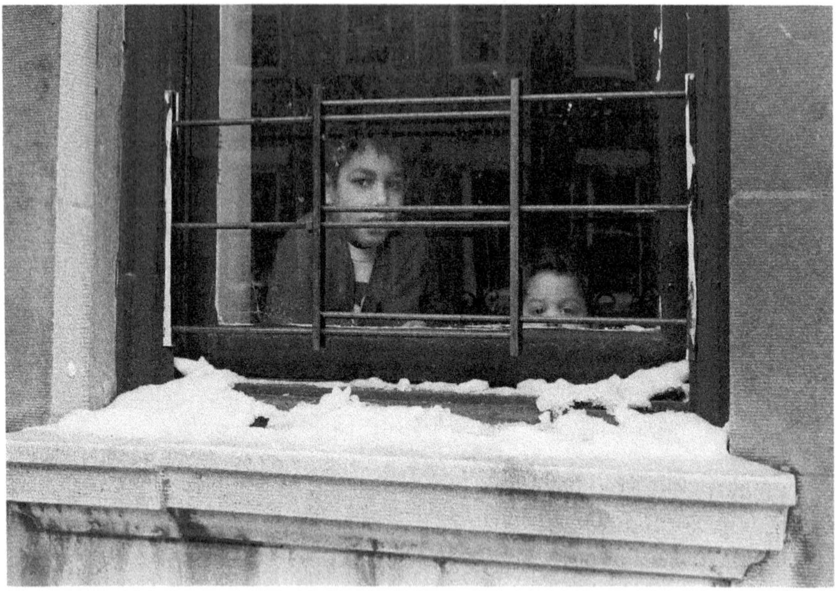

A Child's Declaration of Rights

We recited saccharine prayers,
mother kissed us a pleasant, "Good Night,"
luminous bulbs appeared clandestine
from under our pillows,
we played shadows and bears,
pounced on one another's beds,
or years later turned our baseball radios on;
to imprison and punish the dark
we jabbed at, and poked fun, with lighted wands,
told school-boy riddles,
made up outlandish adventures for long-lost booty
with fantastic ourselves as the heroes.

It's difficult for two energy-laden molecules
to come to a point of rest,
so why do parents banish and sentence
their laughing/grumbling sprites to nethergloom,
pull a shroud over their curious, interactive world?
it is perhaps their most reprehensible crime
to halt cascading sensations
by confining non-criminals
in upstairs darkened, sleep-inducing cells.

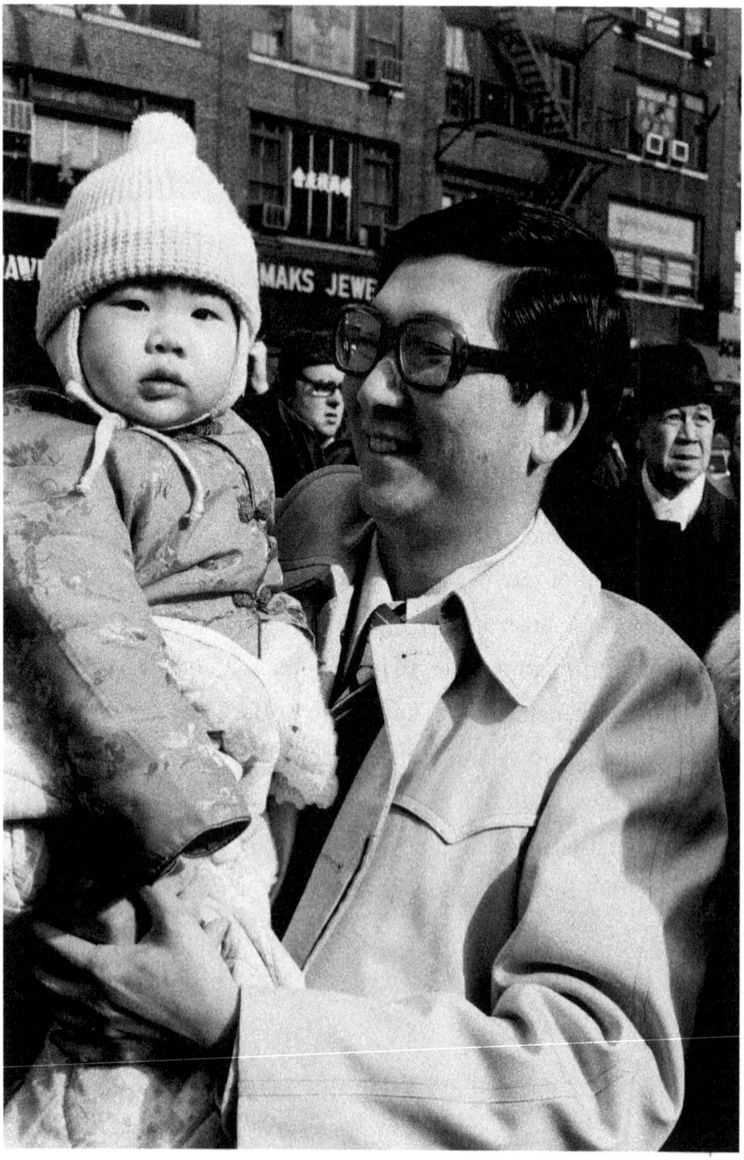
MAKS JEWE

The World According to Da-da

Sleep on, my son,
the world has nowhere to go but down,
there'll be time enough to make your fleeting mark,
study your palimpsest,
learn invigorating new games, sports,
encounter your first enemy,
get jilted by some girl you thought you loved.

You'll have opportunity enough to muff,
lessons to memorize, then disastrously forget,
crowns to win,
fools to flatter,
an envious rabble which must be watched:
you'll need all the strength you can muster
to sequester a few serene hours.

Governments will demand your taxes,
encompass your every move with red-entangling paper,
conscript you into bayonet and fatigues,
then demagogues will cry, "Here's your duty!"
if you object, you'll feel like a Columbia River salmon
fighting against man and the forces of nature.

You'll bury your emotions behind a poker smile,
speak freely to charm an inner coterie,
some days you'll laugh,
more often you'll weep,
defend your core Smalcald principles,
then bend them a little around the edges.

God will sneak up behind your back
and try to overthrow your heart,
finally you'll settle in, mate,
build a wobbly home, seek to make a splash,
improvise a few lullabies for your son
to launch him into the world according to da-da.

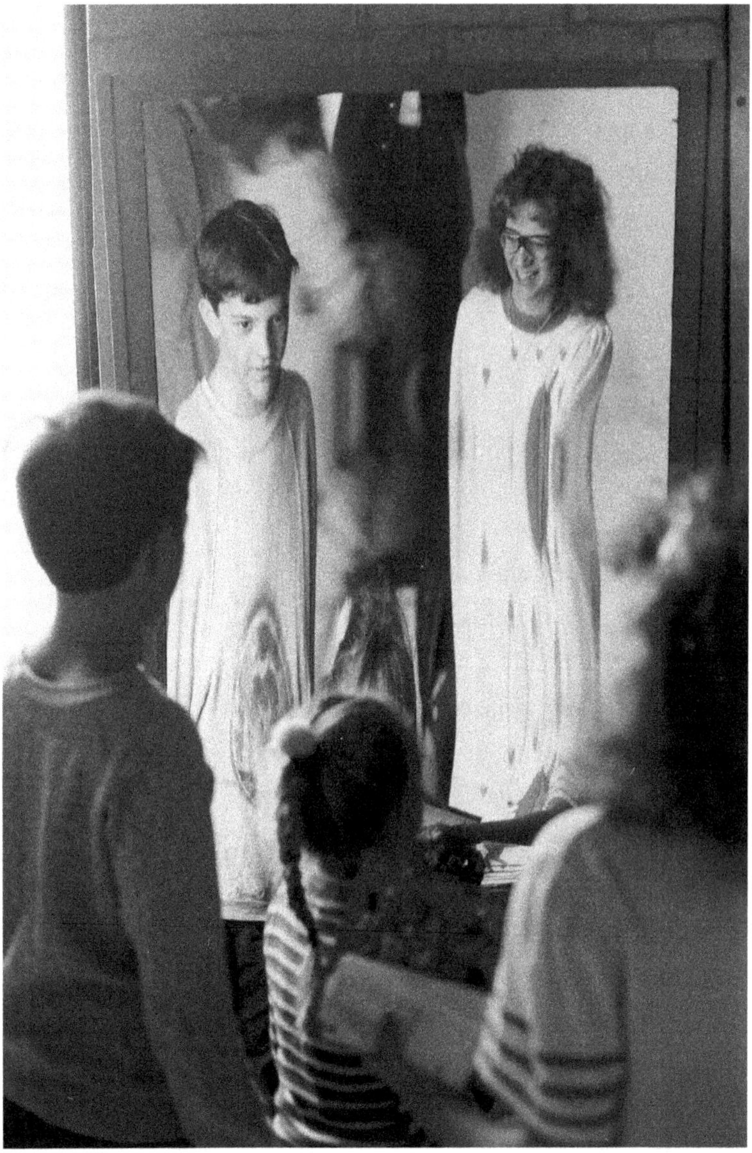

When You're 30

When you're 30, all things jell
or fall apart again,
Eros sublimated by creativity,
fathers reconciled to two-bit sons,
angry young men pacified by this world's goods,
careers solidifying or being born again,
Gentile or Jew, there's no distinction,
God made them both,
they mature the same—
with equal hesitation.

Swimming pool in the suburbs,
missionary passions dropping into familiar grooves,
atrophied limbs jogging
with ten-year-old sons and daughters,
cellophane-wrapped diplomas being
discarded to make room for baby,
fretting about the mortgage unless mommy works,
the same symptoms of ennui
that undid Rome, Carthage, and Babylon.

TV dinner getting cold along the Emmaus Road,
neighbor barricading himself from neighbor,
apocalypse and rumors of eschatology,
far-away images of rusty hair and bloated bodies,
"Won't someone turn up the air conditioning!"
malaise tottering on the precipice of love,
nuclear family subsumed under the *koinonia* of brotherhood?

The past finally coming home to roost,
repressions blow up like firecrackers,
old girlfriends blur into centerfolds,
you're caught in the spiral
of more and more pain to squeeze less and less juice,
spongy marrow growing stiff and squeaky,
apex or nadir—you're free to choose:
roll over dead or hearken to the voice within.

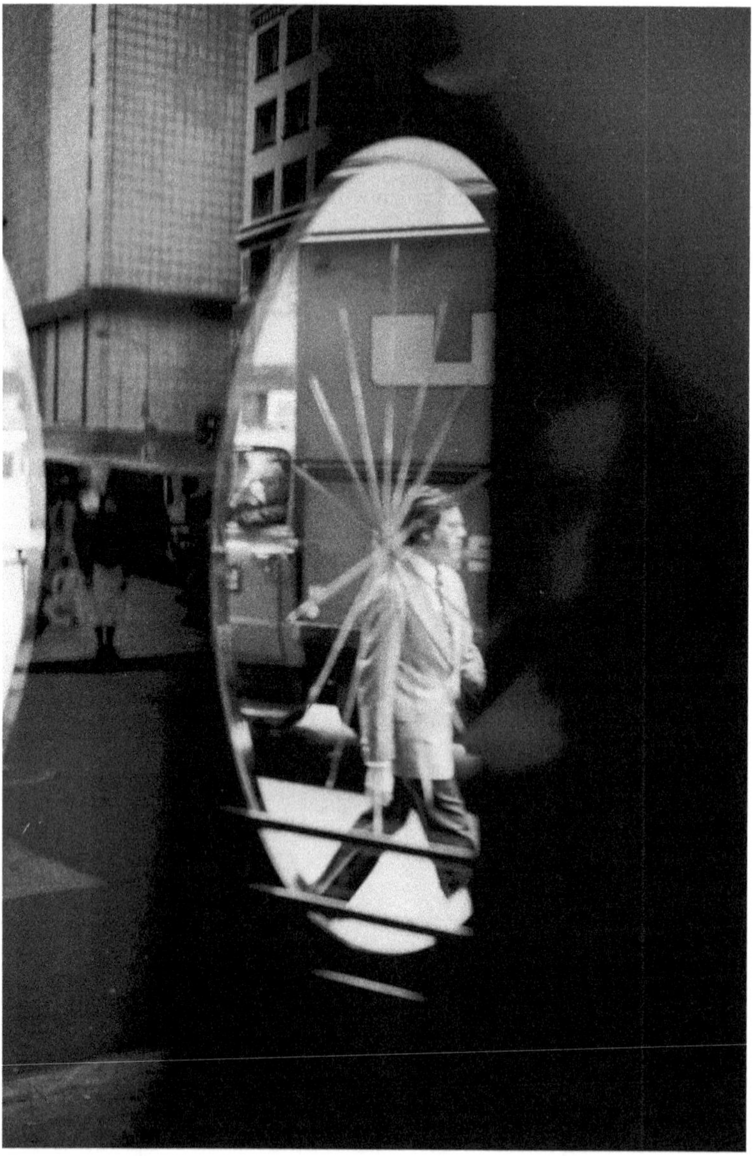

My Frenetic Nerves

The moon is up
and the sun's refracted rays
scorch the evening sky,
a few minutes and all muted colors
will merge into grey.

The crickets tune their mandolins,
lightning bugs glow like magic lanterns,
and a well-deserved calm quiets my frenetic nerves.

I had worked myself into a migraine by mid-afternoon,
and now my urgent hopes seem like petty fantasies,
all I want is:

                                             a glass of milk,
                                   a ham and cheese sandwich,
                               a pillow on which to lay my head.

If I were living far from the nearest metropolis,
perhaps I could follow nature's simple pace,
                      but as it is—blaring engines,
                      hooting whistles,
                      time clocks on every wall
conspire to irritate my stomach and ruin my tempo.

The wife complains I'm cranky,
the children scurry off to the park,
I feel like a fly caught in a concrete web,
the more I struggle, the more I'm encased,
see! gastric juices are already at work.

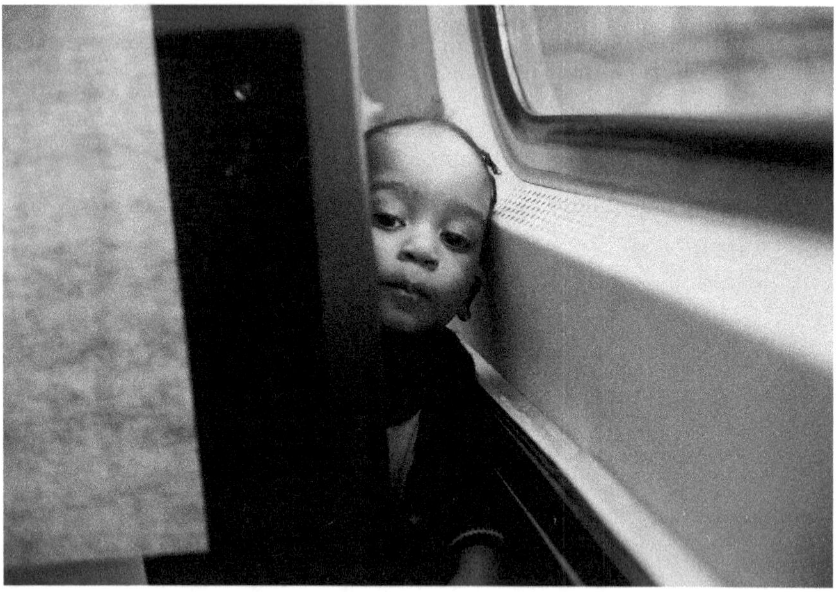

Hush You, Chil'!

Hush you, chil'!
When the sun peeps up, the moon is banished,
Papa'll be home in a minute.
Shall the storm
choose a percussion or woodwind accompaniment?

It's no matter.
He's in Jesus's arms.
As soon as the rains subside,
he'll push on to his shanty,
majestic as a Ferdinand frigate.

Though ol' Pluto nips at his heels
and the stars give birth to delinquent planets,
he's the sturdy sequoia,
more clever than Mr. Lancelot,
that bull's-eye homing sparrow.

Why he so slow, mammy?
I think he want to see me cry.
Honey—no. The night's as impassable as the Nile *sudd*,
the creek bridge prob'ly floatin' downriver,
he doin' all he can to keep from bein' lost.

The candle . . . oh mammy, I'm so scared.
Damnation, chil'! Sing you a rhapsody in rags.
Sit! Walk! Stand!
You ain't needin' nobody.
Why, you' soul's flowin' with milk and honey.

Looky there. I can see his light.
Sure 'nuf. Now two, three, four.
Amen! Bless you, Lazarus.
It's the cock-of-the-rock hisself
as famished and wet as brother Elijah.

Well, if it isn't my two sherbet girls.
Lor', tonight I been down to Lucifer's den
and threw him that emer'ld grail.
Tonight they'll be hanging the Devil in effigy.
Hush! I can hear him yell.

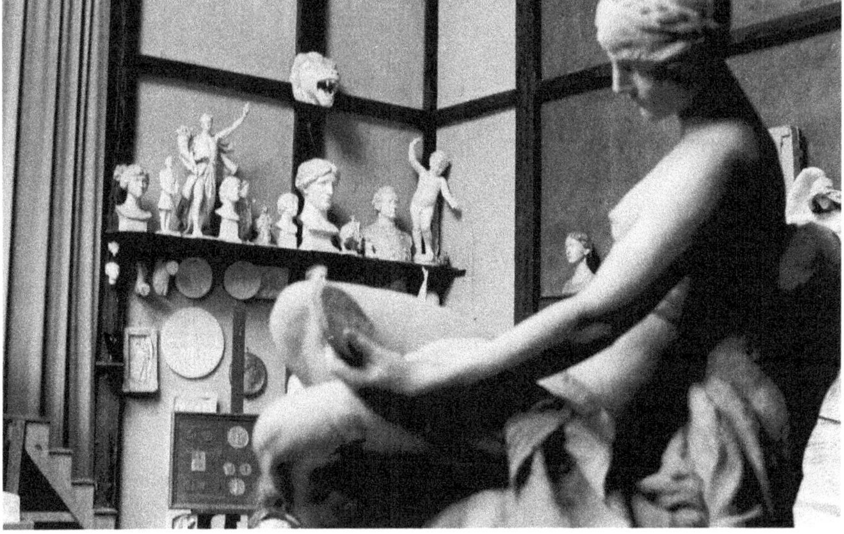

Giving Birth

Pygmalion's marble love
is released by Cupid's chisel.

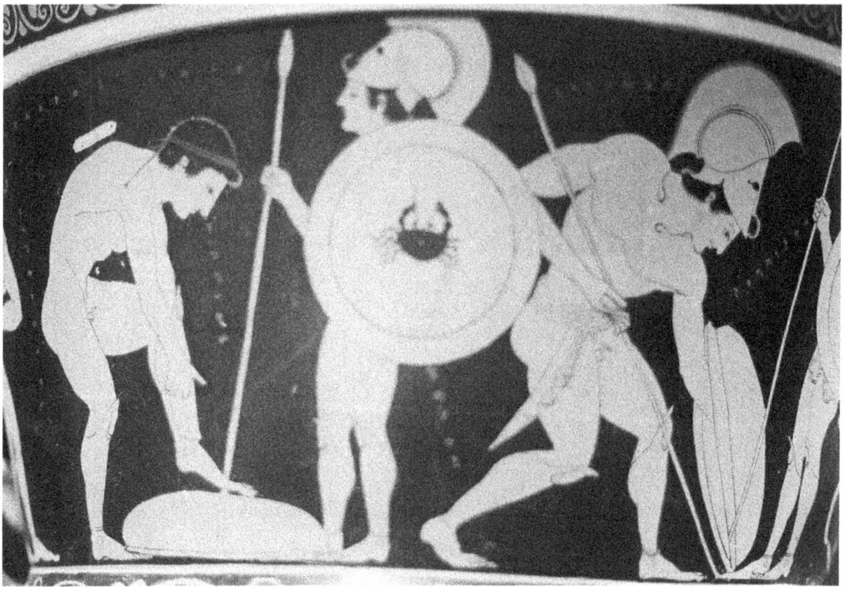

The Judgment of Paris

"To the Most Beautiful"
someone had inscribed on that fateful apple,
to choose between Hera, Athena, and Aphrodite,
the most curvaceous creatures ever formed,
would have put even seer Tiresias at a stuttering loss.

One might win the evening wear or swimsuit competition,
another take honors during the talent show,
a third might answer impromptu questions
with engaging wit and a winning smile,
a panel of distinguished judges was needed

or legal counsel, in case of counter-suit.
Damn it all, if I hadn't been so dazzled
by those fetching under-the-table offers,
Troy might never have lit up the Aegean sky
nor Aeneas fled like a burning brand to mother Rome.

Hector wouldn't have slumped over his vainglorious shield
nor Menelaus crouched inside that wooden, equestrian present.
why me? why should a peace-loving herdsman,
who never did anyone harm (save for a few ravenous wolves),
inadvertently cause the greatest battle of our time?

Maybe I should have cut up the apple into three equivalent prizes,
though I'm not sure that would have satisfied any;
or I might have declined the invitation,
but I've always lived by impulse,
and only, of late, come to regret the rashness of my youth.

Some say time is a two-way river;
perhaps I could paddle back upstream
and decide again—a wiser, saner future,
but one day life hurled out a gleaming apple,
and like a wayward sunfish I bit the most voluptuous bait.

And, oh, those incredible few nights I had
on the lemonwood divan with delectable Helen,
before cries of "To battle!" "Take up arms!"
I wasn't tipsy, nor am I really a bad sort.
You philosophers, how would you decide?

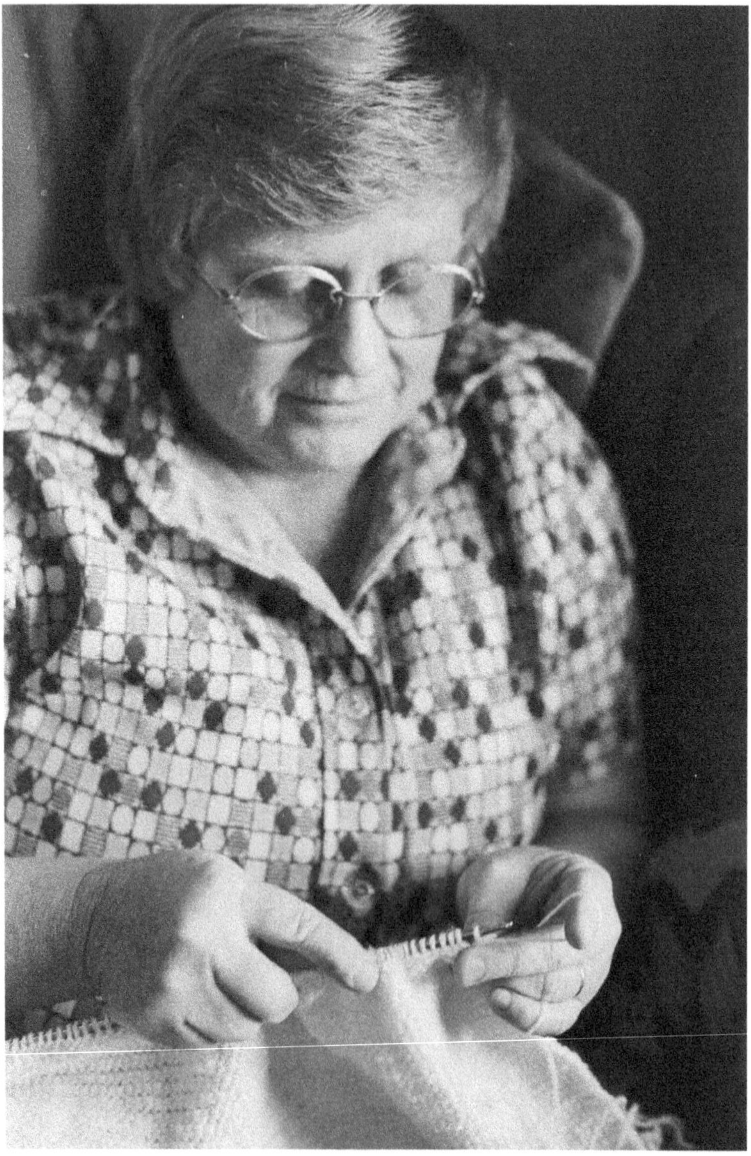

Penelope

Penelope, fend off your faithless suitors,
each night undo
> what you labored at
> the day before—
> beneath unsuspecting eyes.
Only he who pulls back Ulysses' bow
can sleep with his regal consort.

Telemachus and that swineherd
twinkle at your perplexity
and still the childhood scar
startles his old nurse.

You feel the pinch of Clotho's noose
struggling against the die cast,
yet your man will overturn the tables,
and you can finish this Homeric tapestry
as soon as you let that beggar through the door.

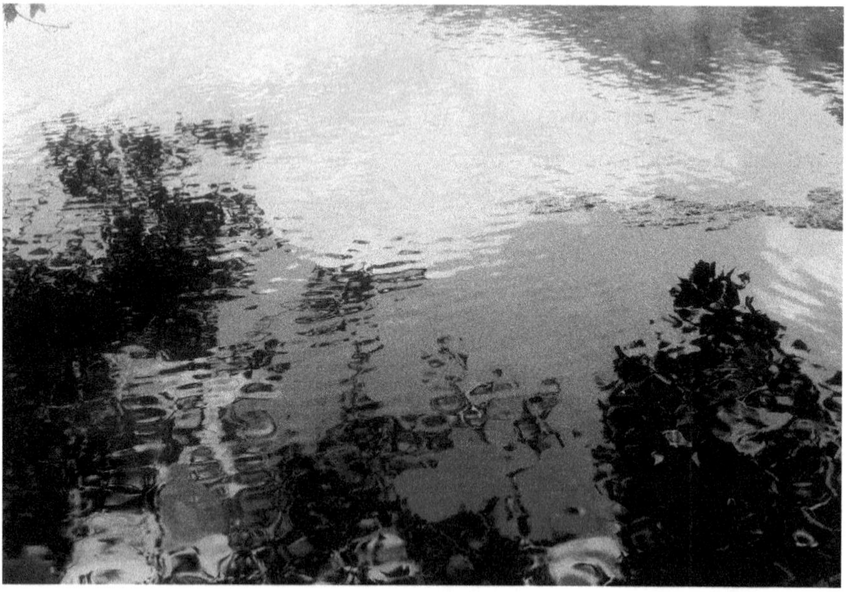

Echo, the Nymph

Poor, garbled Echo
—whose Narcissus she longs for
with furtive flats and sharps—
resembles a melancholy mirror,
excites no sparks of incandescence,
just blue, unflattering imitation.

Static, directional Echo
murmuring name upon lover's name,
like a doppelgänger gong
or a Barbie with pull-down strings,
her voice is low, muffled, subdued
like a Delft earthenware *vanitas*.

Sputtering, fading Echo,
much like Achilles bereft of Patroclus,
avenges love by sulking by a pool,
spins her beeswax gramophone
with its scratchy, bent disk,
while sitting unrequited on the banks of Acheron.

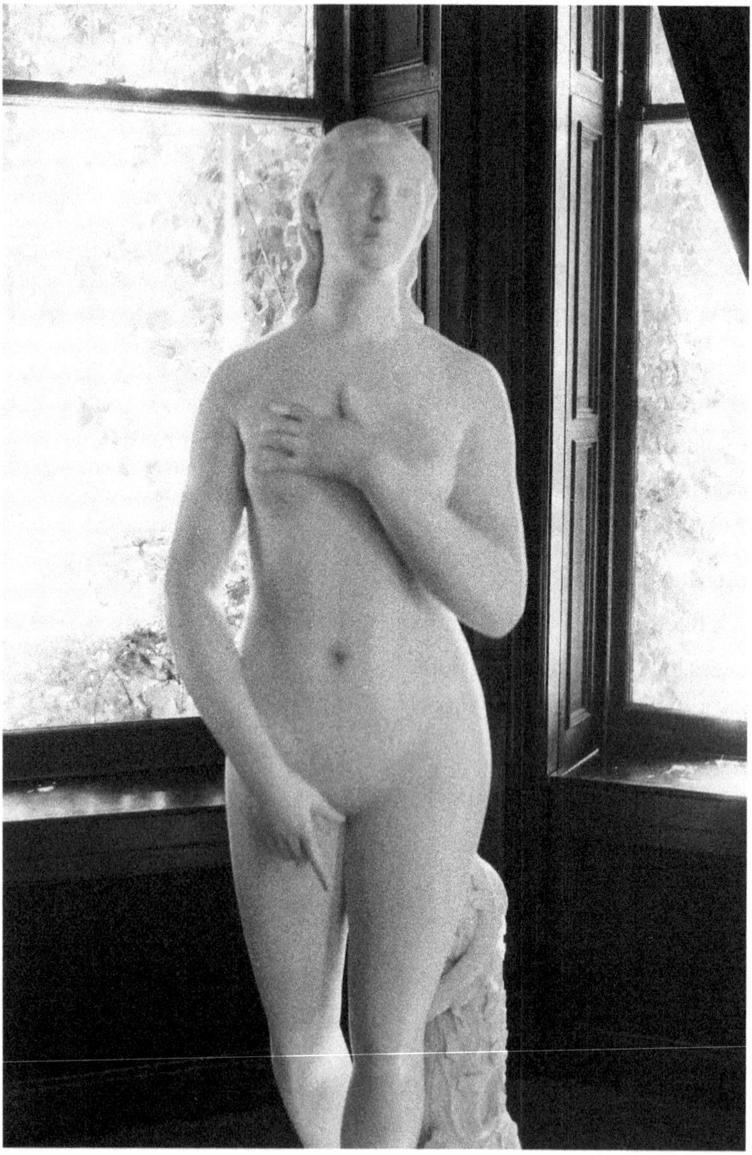

Venus

Irresistible as Venus,
burning Cupid's silly arrows.

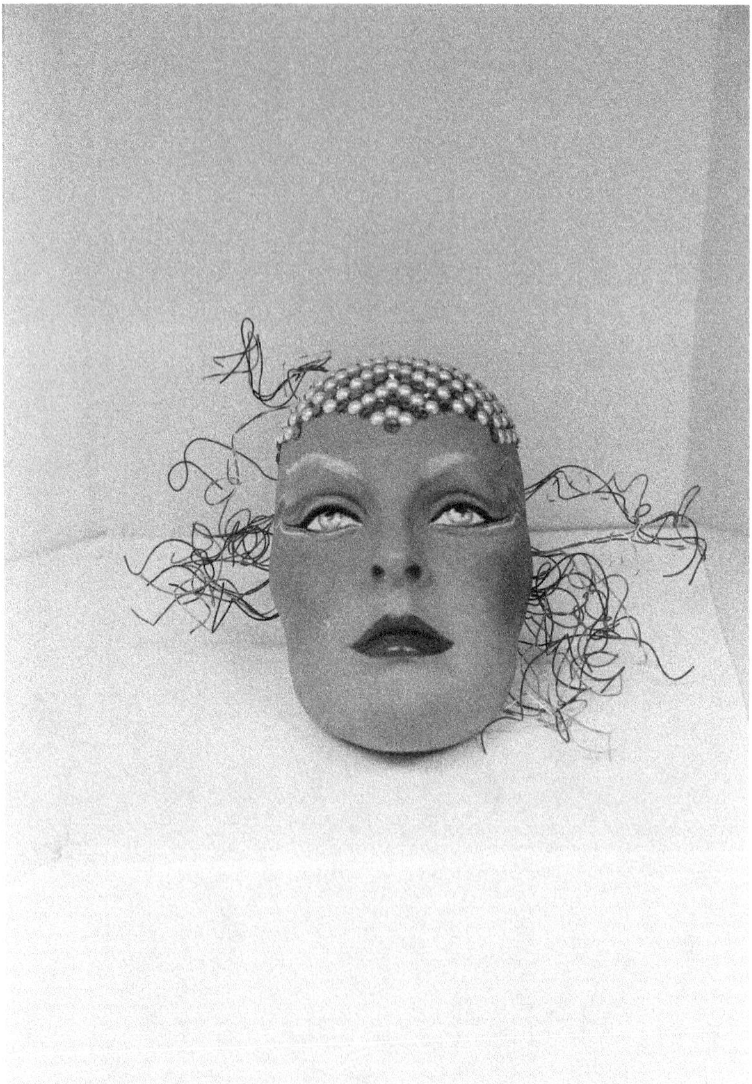

Medea with her Medusa Head

Escaping with the golden fleece,
leaving King Aeëtes far behind,
Medea with her Medusa head,
potent Colchic medicines
to brighten our Argonaut jamboree.

I suspected nothing
but a woman tired of dreary
surroundings and settled routine,
a few frightful herbs, hex sign
armbands, fits of abject depression.

I was enamored of barbaric,
unwhitened features,
harsh, cloying phonemes,
the romance of conquest,
but forgot about raising babies.

I was so sure I could reform the conjurer
with high Grecian values,
a husband's firm, unswaying hand,
could enlighten her uncultured lineage
with Anaximander, Thales, and Heraclitus.

Maybe the centaur was right, after all,
you can pass through the clashing rocks but once
—unscathed—don't press your Argonaut luck,
old dragons don't die so easily.

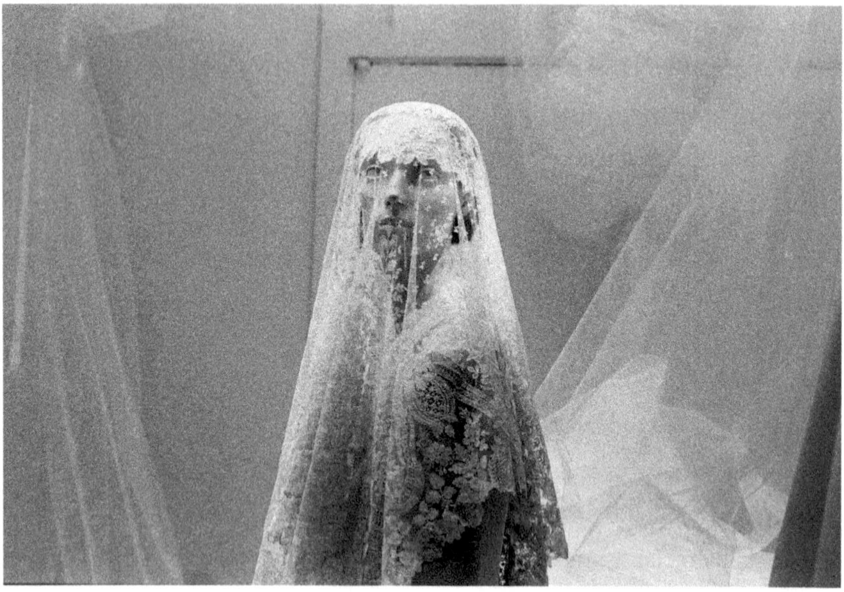

Abram's Quandary

More beautiful . . .
than Abram's wife,
who seduced the sceptered Pharaoh?
her wrap-around, distilled proportions
more sinuous than Nefertiti's,
a wanton Helen smile,
talcum powder cheeks,
that French-kiss entangling tongue
driving a patriarch to concealment.

A bashful, bare, opened breast
succulent as Tokay clusters
ripening into a skin tone centerfold,
the come-on, hazel pools, gleaming, white-
arrow teeth, the carnelian sucking depths,
unbridled tresses playing peek-a-boo
as coral kissing gourami,
flapping nightshade fragrance
—enough to doom a pecking bird.

The brows (arched and penciled thin),
lobes of moon snail pearl,
two alabaster columns expanding
gently upward from the five-toed base
into a penis-desirous silk girdle,
those scheming, unending thighs
like forked walking sticks
leading a blind bear
into a crotch of honey.

He stands perplexed:
shall he enter triumphant through the open, bulging gates
or grab the bulbous outer rungs
and mount a more vulnerable, rear attack?
No matter—one can imagine Abram
trying ever so hard to people Israel
for sixty-semen years,
no doubt an irksome, ulcer-inducing task,
yet would he have it any other way?

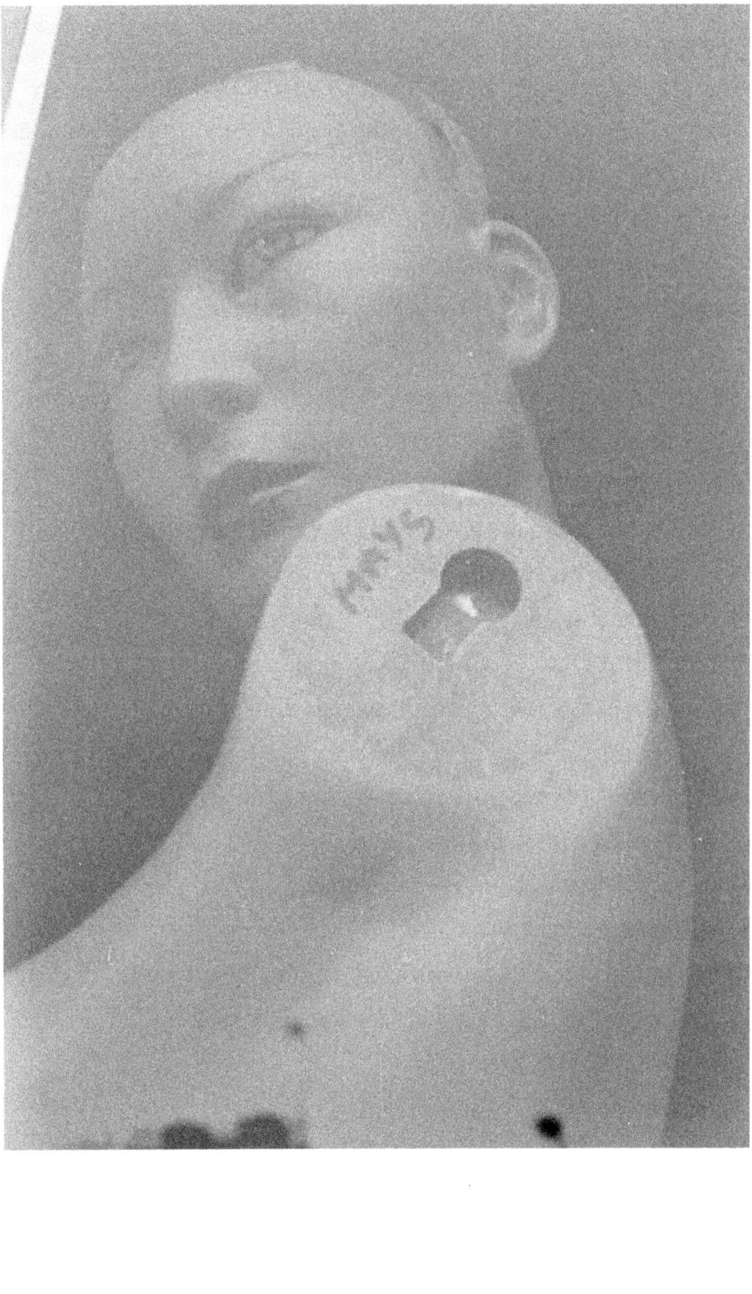

Hosea

God commanded me, Hosea, to form a liaison,
marry a strumpet, defend those who have no champion,
as a shivering/trembling prophet
I gather "Not My People," give birth to "Not My Children,"
while remaining faithful to wives with a thousand idolatrous paramours,
who consort in sacred groves and high, blaspheming places,
following after rotund, lascivious Ashtoreth,
dancing naked before stone phalluses and ivory pudenda,
mingling chosen chromosomes in alien double-helix bonds.

Away, my lustful, reprobate people
who eat raisin cakes and offerings to renegade gods,
I am your one true husband,
who demolishes Assyrian harems and Canaanite temple prostitutes,
I form a wedge between body and spirit
in all who are not Israel,
who frolic like promiscuous baboons,
despoiling the sacred love nest for a moment's pleasure.

I'll have no more of your furtive, one-night embraces,
we've an eternal plighted troth,
broken, but reset by soul-sincere repentance,
I'm a jealous, seething lover,
swift to forgive, wooing back with small talk
and memorable caresses, I am your one and only man,
all others are desperate pretenders.

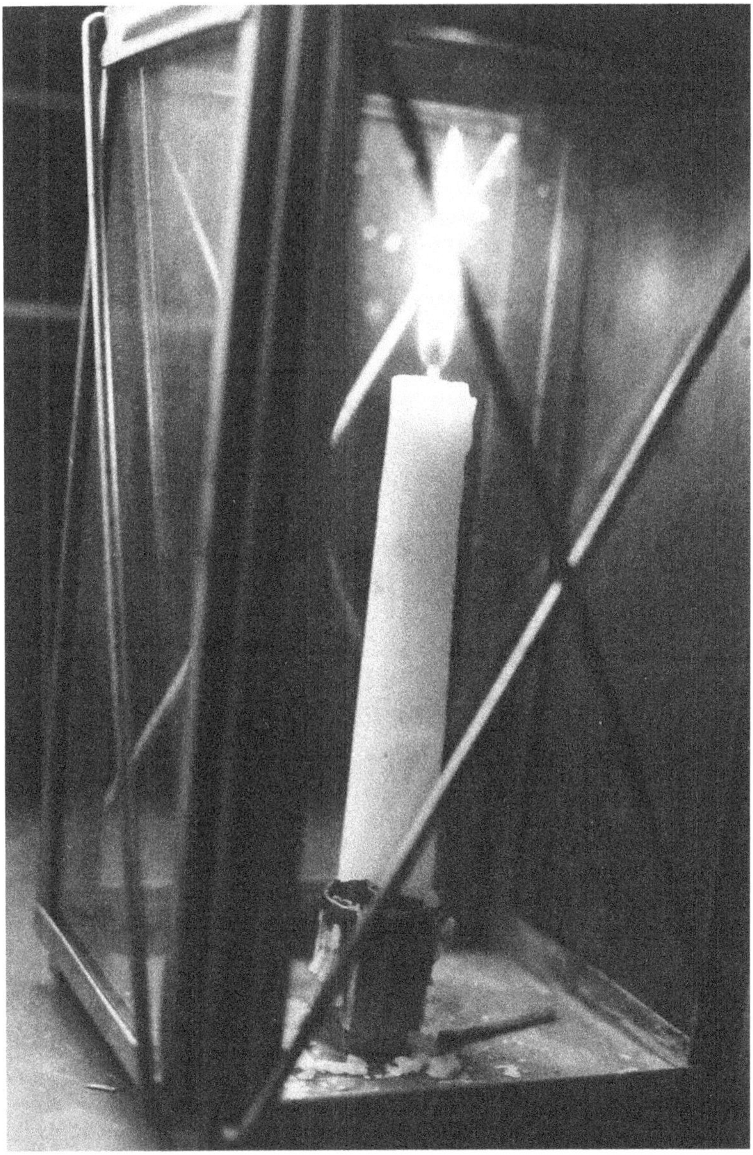

The foolish virgins

unprepared for their lover's reluctance,
wait nervously like erotic Spanish nuns,
        fans blink,
        eyes wink,
a petticoat raised ever so slightly.

Their hearts roaring
like a four-alarm fire,
        could he be assaying
        some inferior rival?
Their oil runs low,
    so in haughty retreat
        they make a great to-do.

They flaunt their ribald indifference,
take their merry time
to spank his ingratitude,
        while some shout, "Wait till dawn!"
        head off for two or three candles.
To their utter shock,
        he's courted some low-class broad,
        shunned a marriage of convenience:
how could he escape their net?

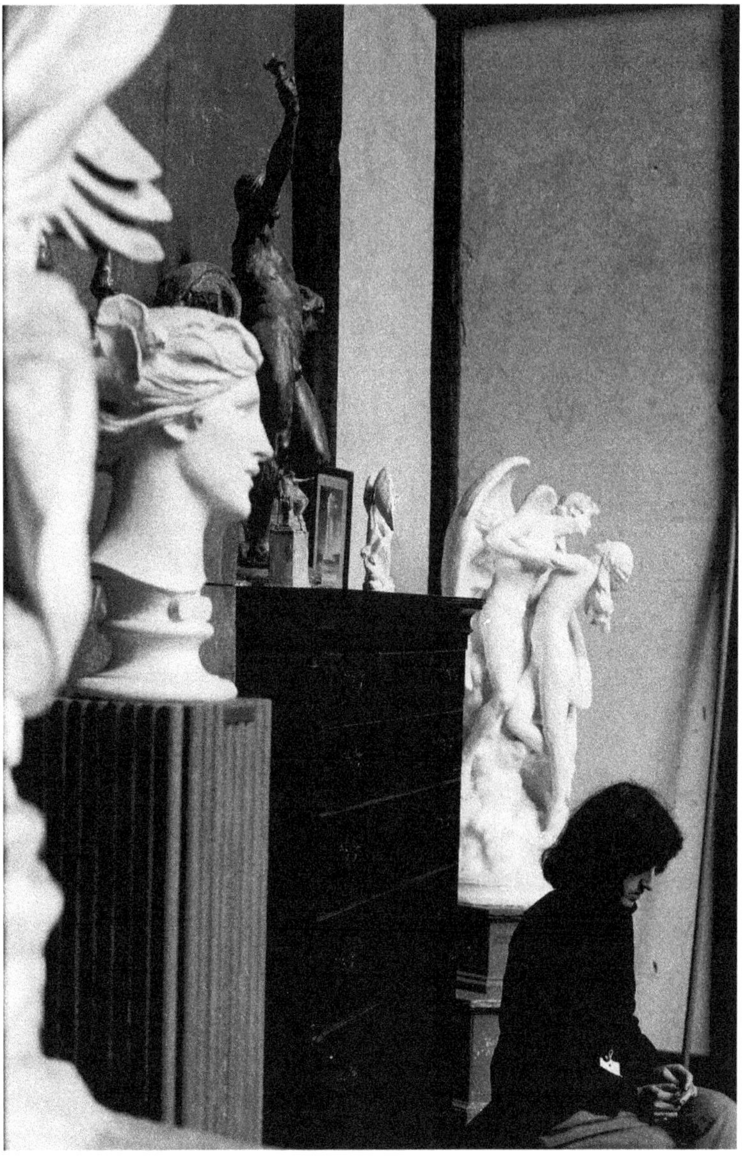

A la John of the Cross

When I remove my ethereal veil,
purse these pomegranate lips,
your kisses grow steamy, spiced,
much as Ruth toying with Boaz's toes,
who arched her coy back on the cut alfalfa
anxious for a serendipitous encounter.

My feverish senses can be aroused
by a glance, a whisper, a wink,
I long to inhale your intoxicating presence
till it palpitates my panting pores,
then I'll be satiated as a Shulammite nymph
whose proffered key unlocked door after nubile door.

Intimacy lingers, lullabies reassure,
I sigh through crescendo after crescendo
of purgation, illumination, union,
the body stands seamless as the soul
on the threshold of some culminating metamorphosis,
all aglow with uncreated photons.

Let me savor your tongue, then your full mouth,
as I abandon myself to ecstatic fingers,
all aquiver for deep exploratory thrusts,
I become mucous, orgasmic:
Yes! Yes! Yes!
enveloped in a supertactile, all-encompassing kind of love.

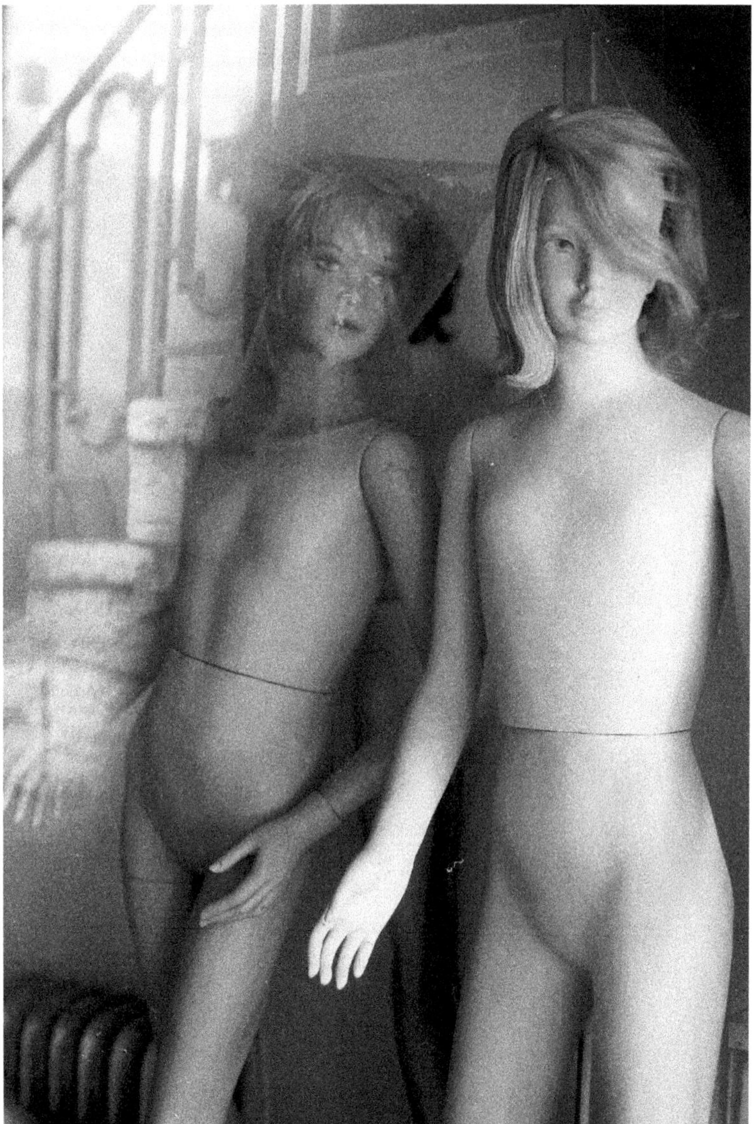

Two Nude Virgins

The saint who slept between two nude virgins,
neither converted nor deflowered one.

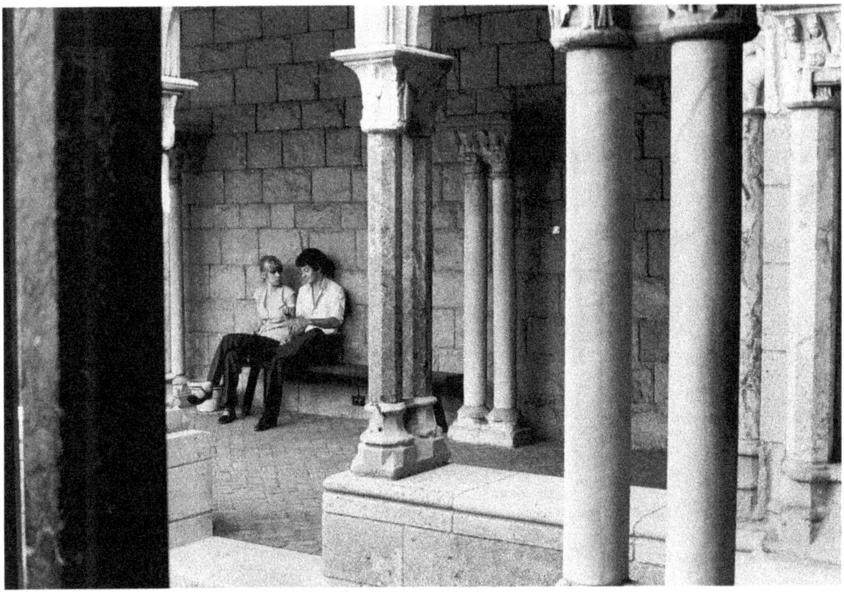

a *Charis* all can partake of

Would that the world convalesced,
its wounds healed,
pain was transposed into felicity,
you and I stood still.

Today the sky rippled across our bow,
you registered Fahrenheit,
unpainted oars plied away care,
our kissing sequence outlasted Ingrid Bergman's.

Passions skyrocketed and then burst out loud,
your picnic basket sailed home full,
our hands whispered, stuttered
—I made you laugh.

Pillowed up against my shoulder,
Ruth gleaning her Boaz,
Heloise cradled in Abelard's arms,
—a meadowlark anthem, a finch serenade.

Moments to turn saints green,
like the calm after intercourse
or a vibrant Gothic beam,
the joy of intermission—with two acts to go.

Will you come then two abreast
into this refitted Dilmun,
a Sabbath for the unbaptized,
a *Charis* all can partake of.

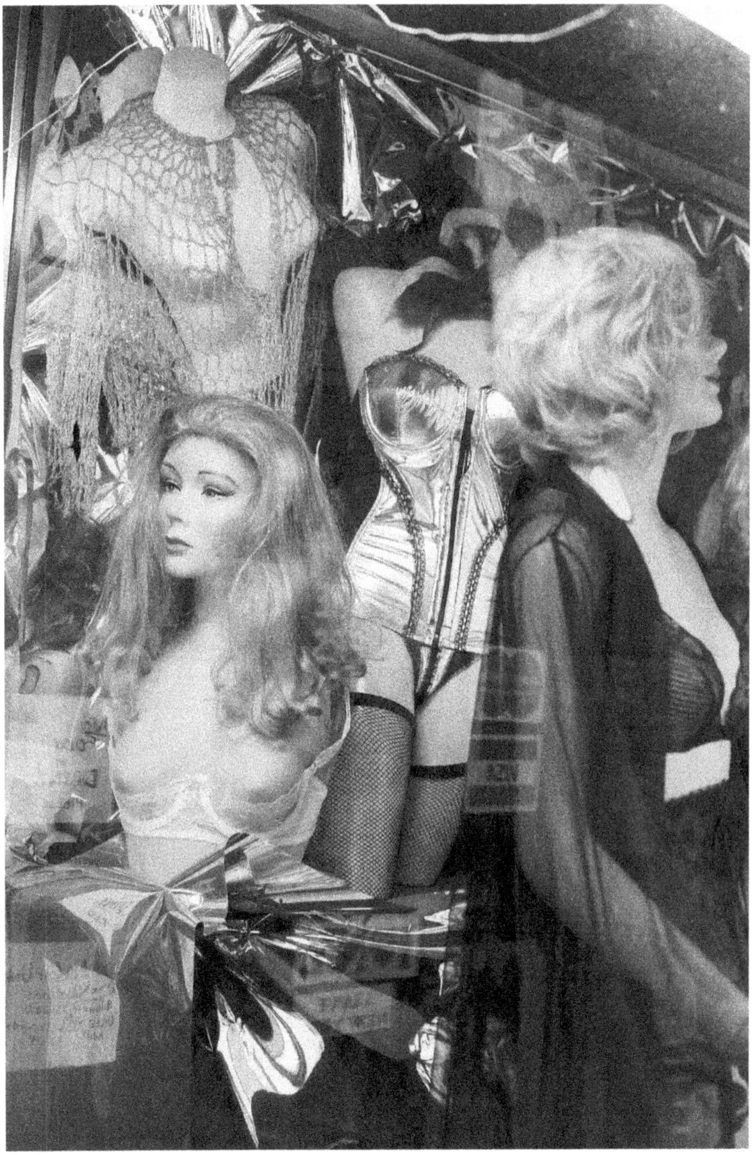

Au Naturel

I've enough of rosy red
        and whited mums,
panting after seductive thighs,
        star-struck at the black holes of your retinas.

Liquid rouge makes me want to puke,
        pantyhose disfigures your skin tones,
bawdy paraphernalia gives me stomach cramps,
        pink or purple bulbs bewilder my erotic sense.

Au naturel appeals to me,
        no eau de cologne or lacy lingerie,
the mind paints its own perfection,
        props are unnecessary.

Don't give me your pulp-novel vocabulary,
        goose bumps or loss of appetite,
emotional seesaws or ecstatic delirium
        —mating isn't the new world, nor are boyfriends Adamic bliss.

Go in like the Oriental with the kettle barely warm,
        I'd as soon halt celestial motion,
fix the ecliptic of the wandering star,
        as plug love as an end-all.

For a heart's unbreakable except you drop it,
        the sinews are elastic, supple;
what a fearful portent
        to put Aphrodite on a pedestal.

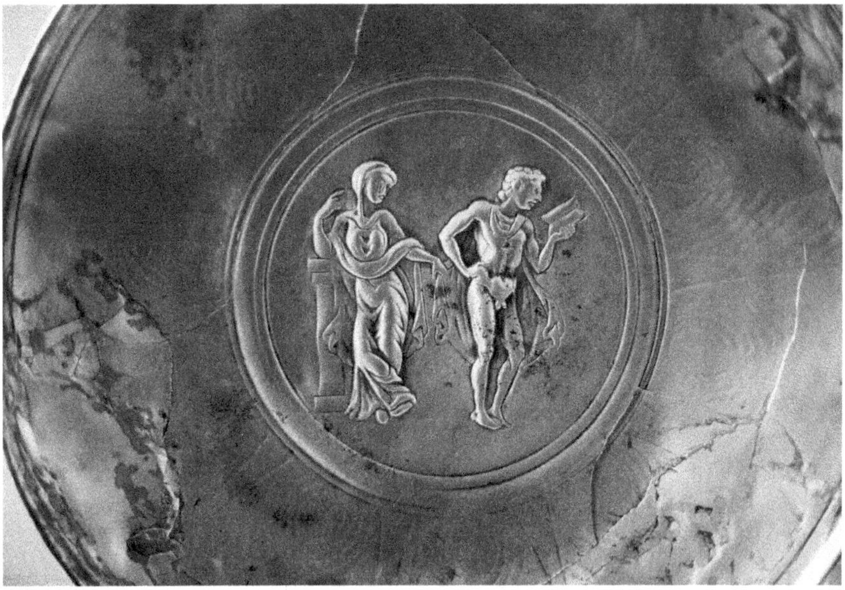

Satisfying a Poet

How can I satisfy a poet's needs?
with the sestet chiasmus
of my sprung-verse hips?

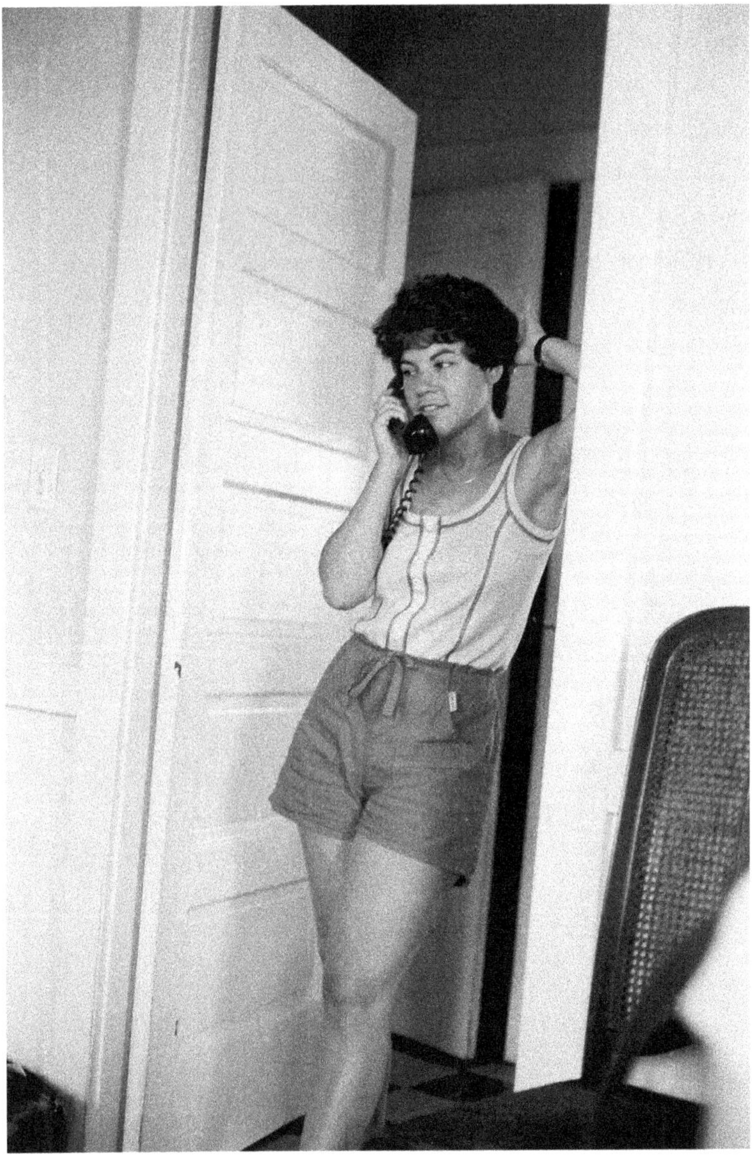

Near Dejection

I cried for more cymbals

—only heard grating tympani,

I commanded the infantry to move forward

but up came the tanks,

I sighed for *otium sanctum*,

then someone blared out in quadraphonic stereo,

I longed for an afternoon of bedroom indelicacies,

and fortuitously my wife responded with coquettish, college girl fervor.

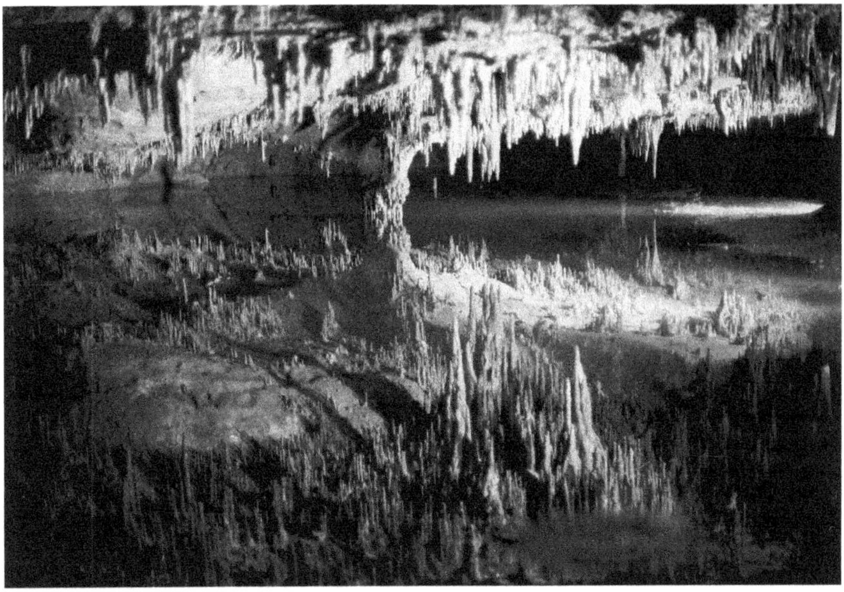

The Stone Woman

Your body, my dear, is a jagged peak,
all angles and points,
I cut myself on your basalt outcroppings,
my chest is sore from your needle-like stings,
your lizard back is prickly, corrugated,
your legs hard as amber,
at your thighs where the timberline stops—
what a view of metamorphosed boulders!

When I climb to the top of your naked crags,
that navel is a rhyolite cavern,
your rump—separated by plate tectonics—
in your mouth are dripping stalactites and stalagmites,
your nose is a miniature Matterhorn,
below the mossy clumps of your brows
are piercing cat's-eye tourmaline
inset by rutile inclusions.

Your lobes are water contoured
into potholes and escarpments,
your feet resemble trilobites,
your fingers jut out like strands of milky quartz;
from this geological description, my dear,
people might assume you to be some stone monster out of Daniel,
instead, you're a soft, fleshly cushion
and I rest my head in a pleasingly freckled hollow.

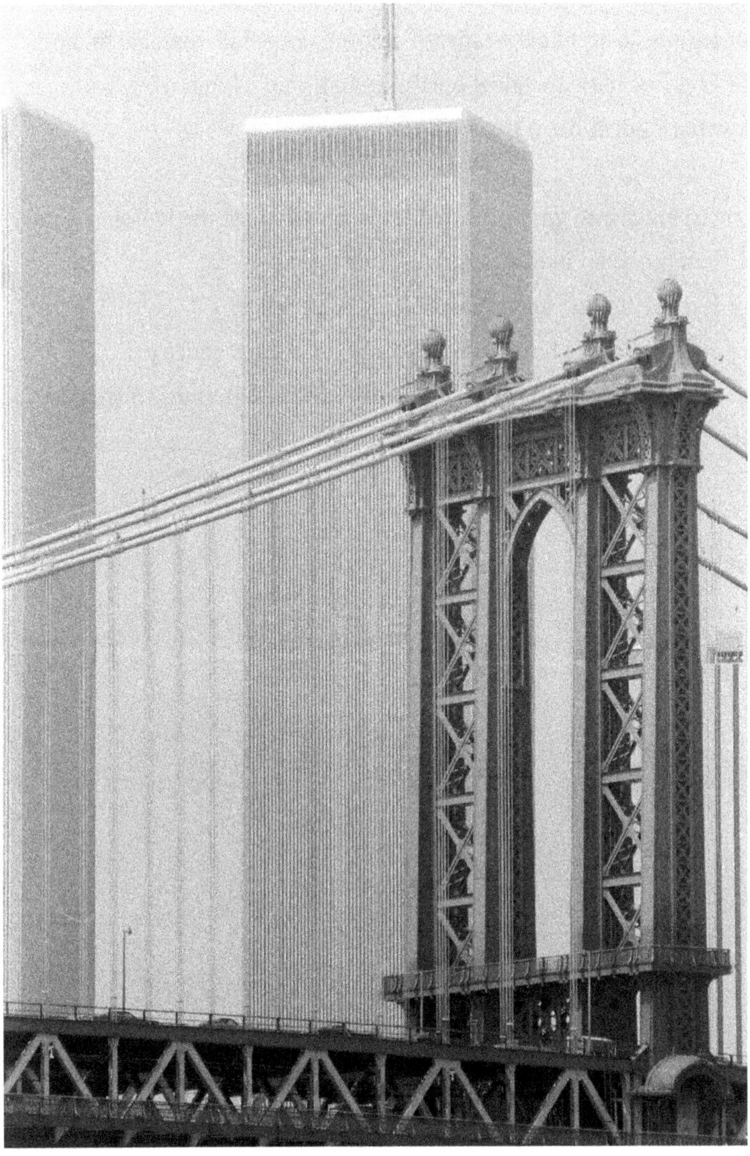

Erotic Architecture

Your breasts are like twin high-rise towers,
your nose, the arch of a Roebling suspension bridge,
your legs descend like the tapered columns of a Palladian Parthenon,
your eyes resemble the glass portholes in a ship of concrete,
below the midriff lies a sinkhole auditorium.

I long to enter into your bowered archway, slip past the inviolate gate,
your bangs glisten like burnished copper,
your feet are tucked under like Chippendale paws,
your ankles like the Ionic volutes of a neo-classical transept,
the semi-circular vaulting of your marble back demands a Sistine fresco,
may I flip open your *belles heures*?

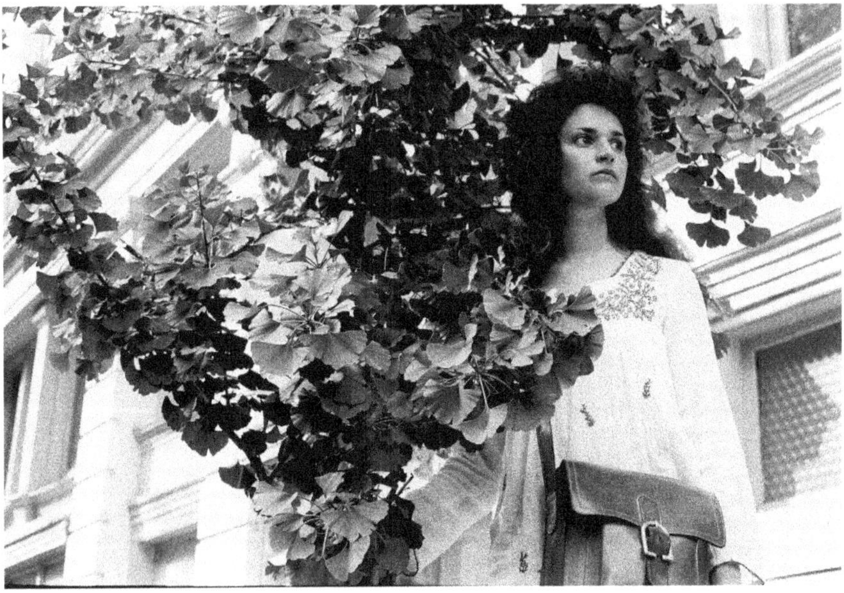

You, a Gazelle

You stand there—a sweet-smelling gazelle—
skin of amber, limbs of bronze,
bounding into my arms like a sure-footed fawn,
licking salt from my proffered lips,
you romp about on all fours,
first on your delectable stomach, then on your ecstatic back,
I'm helpless before your mottled features,
you caper about majestic as a slow-motion sequence,
leapingly light, blushing as the rosy-fingered dawn.

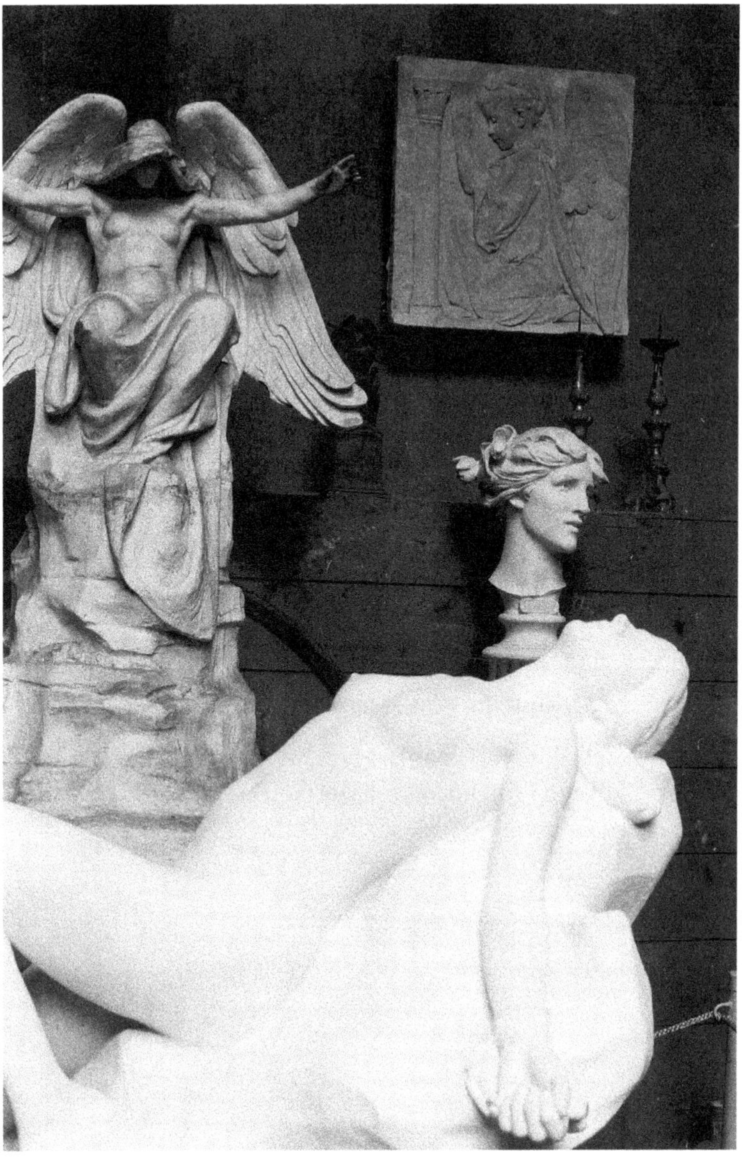

Nakedness in the Morning

Nakedness in the morning—
how wet, voluptuous, and satisfying
compared to midnight's bland embrace,
the sun dances on the sinews of the skin
casting its yellowish glance on exposed contours,
though the imagination is less sharp,
the eye pencils in, lingers over charged detail,
two planes intersect in ribald acrobatic maneuvers;
so many angles, degrees of penetration
as to bewilder even the geometer's protractor and compass,
strange visceral cluckings,
erotic phrases ripped out of steamy copybooks,
dark, uninhibited chic
overcome by teasing, enticing day.

Some make love to remember in vivid hues,
others block out the picturesque, concrete,
cling to feverish chiaroscuro isles of meaning,
a few copulate for surer union,
others surge forward in an uncontrollable biologic urge with no psychic
    attachment,
then all nudity unravels,
it's far better to caress at sunrise—
the first encounter with a promise of living Technicolor.

oes It Again!

SOCIETY

Brooke
PRETTY BABY
Shields
Interview

Exclusive Profile &
Topless Nude Centerfold
Of World's Most Popular
Covergirl!

ON SALE NOW

Mermaids on Land?

Why, what do mermaids do on land
after their dorsal fins have been removed,
but walrus-strut from pond to pool
to prevent scaly dehydration.

Mucus gills clog up due to excess nitrogen,
since their equilibrium's been disturbed outside their liquid element,
thus many have succumbed to sedatives and barbiturates:
cinematic bombshells prone to self-immolation.

Normally mermaids dally, exposed on crags above the foaming waves,
and so derange the leering seafarer,
since any male worth his salt is duly frustrated
by aroused breasts and no viable means of consummation.

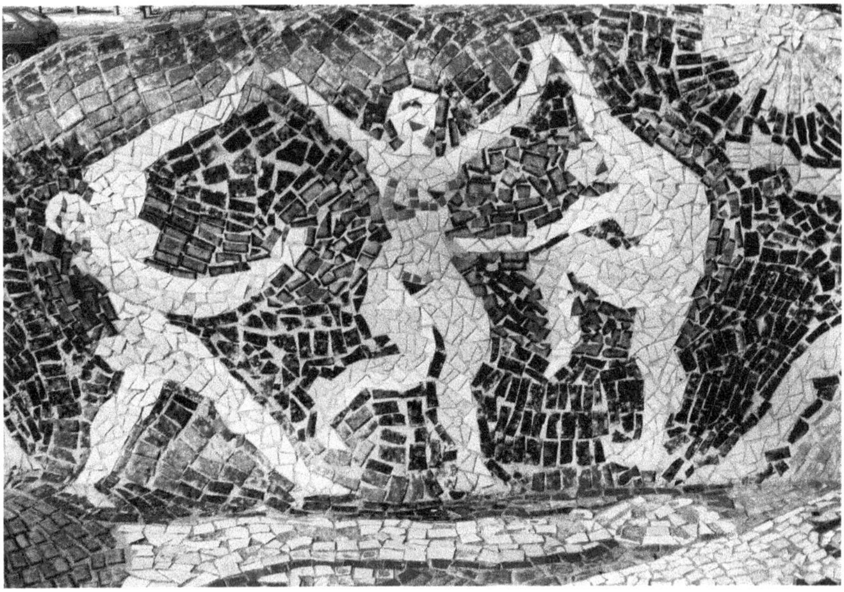

The Hollow Suburbs

We live in the hollow suburbs
between each other's thighs,
you with lustrous, dangling breasts,
me with a roaming, unstoppable priapus;
overexcited at each inadvertent turn of flesh,
we jump the neighbor's fence,
what harm can there be in infidelity
since contraceptives never fail?
let's spice up this bland palate,
since commitment's a shrunken relic of some more chivalrous age.

What is life? a coiled embrace,
a skin-to-skin interlude, a lengthening orgasm,
for souls to touch is a mystic's hallucination,
I would be false to my own id
if I didn't reconnoiter;
all I know is that following perfunctory foreplay,
animals mount up for culmination,
to allow penetration is a form of consent;
thus hedonism thrives—on sheer self-flattery.

Son of man, have you observed this coquetry,
the intrigues, this mastery of the arts of self-deception,
every person appearing as a Casanova or a Cleopatra
in his own distorted erotic mirror?

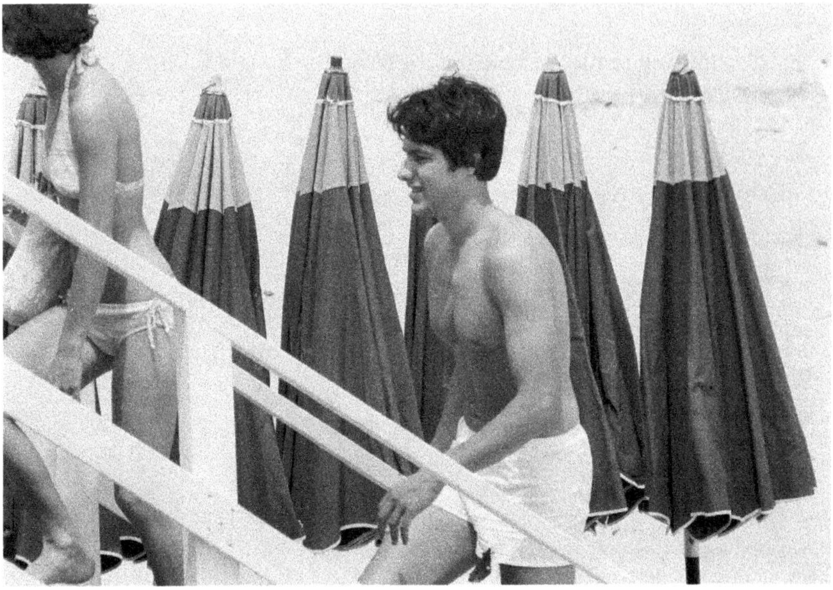

Keep Away from Knives

Keep away from knives
or any enchantress with alluring eye shadow;
should she unveil her couched splendor,
you're entangled in coiffure loops,
sparkling, ebullient laughter,
entranced by glistening lips, svelte incisors,
overcome by a most charming vulnerability,
clinging arias,
that murmuring rivulet of synchronized need.

Beware the underside of razors—
you're cut before you're aware;
neither wink at some languorous piece of flesh,
nor squeeze the statuesque exterior,
nor gaze inadvertently down a loosened bodice,
or else you could end up swallowed inside a yawn
or be crushed between two omnipresent nipples.

If you're gaga for the swaying skirt,
you're likely to be suffocated by a boa's minuet,
its scales overwhelm any who are overcurious and headstrong.

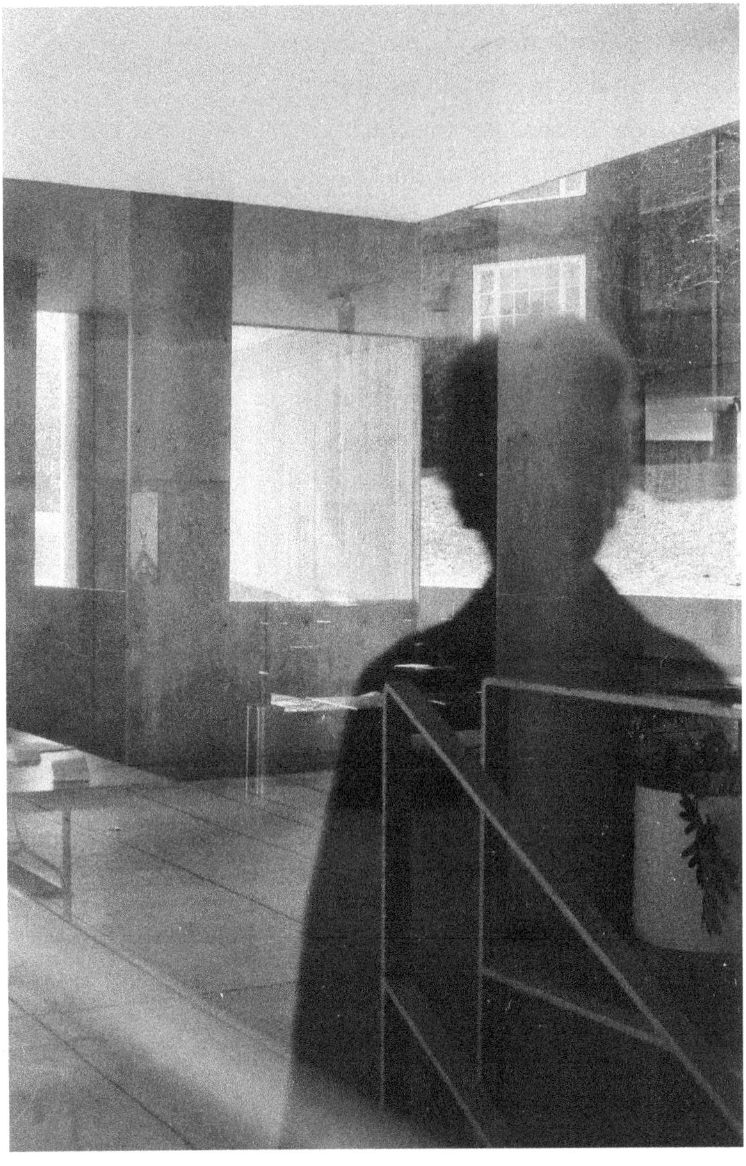

She Entered the Blue, Virginal Sky

She entered the blue, virginal sky
as a fledgling bud about to unfurl,
her luminous corolla was so fragrantly exposed
that rivals wilted from envy and disdain,
however, soon she came slithering back—
cut, bleeding, whimpering with child,
having been poked by some overbearing Judas,
now she crawls, hugging the sepia-slit earth.

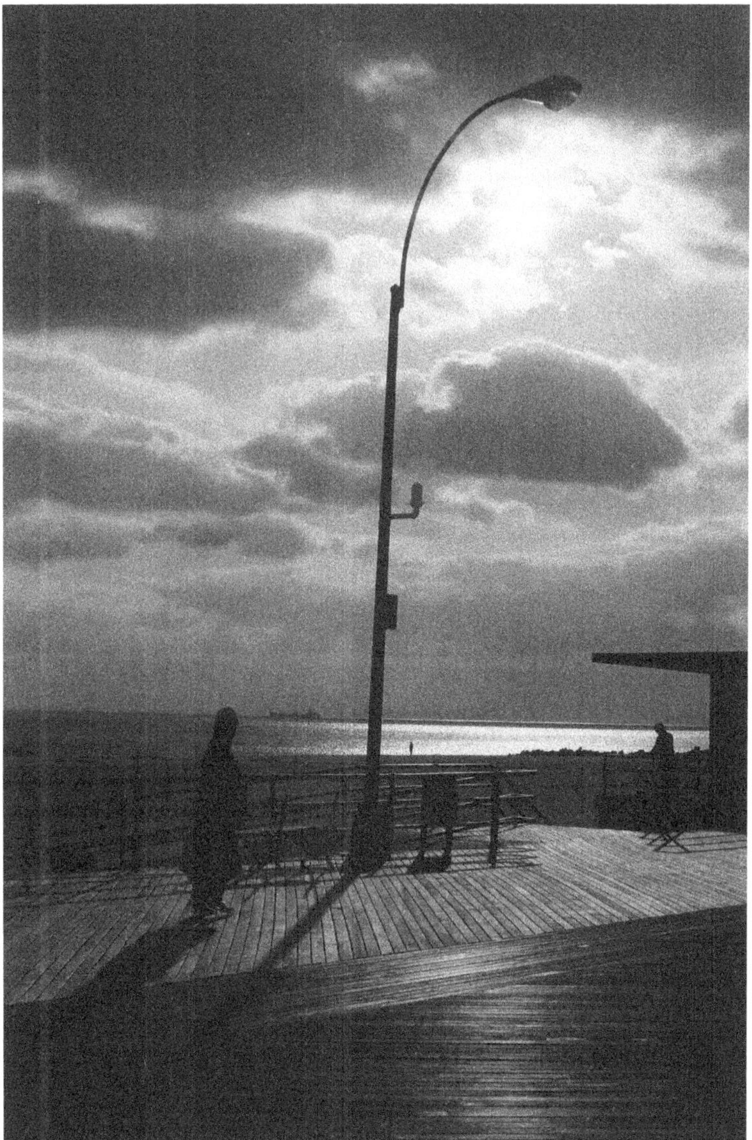

Promiscuity

I am big with a child!
Having kissed the morning star,
made love to the setting sun,
dallied with the lecherous moon,
run my fingers down Jupiter's spine,
whispered sweet nothings to Mars,
trembled at Pluto's frigid score,
I was in ecstasy over half the Milky Way,
then hid my bulging womb from all-devouring Saturn.
But who was the real daddy?

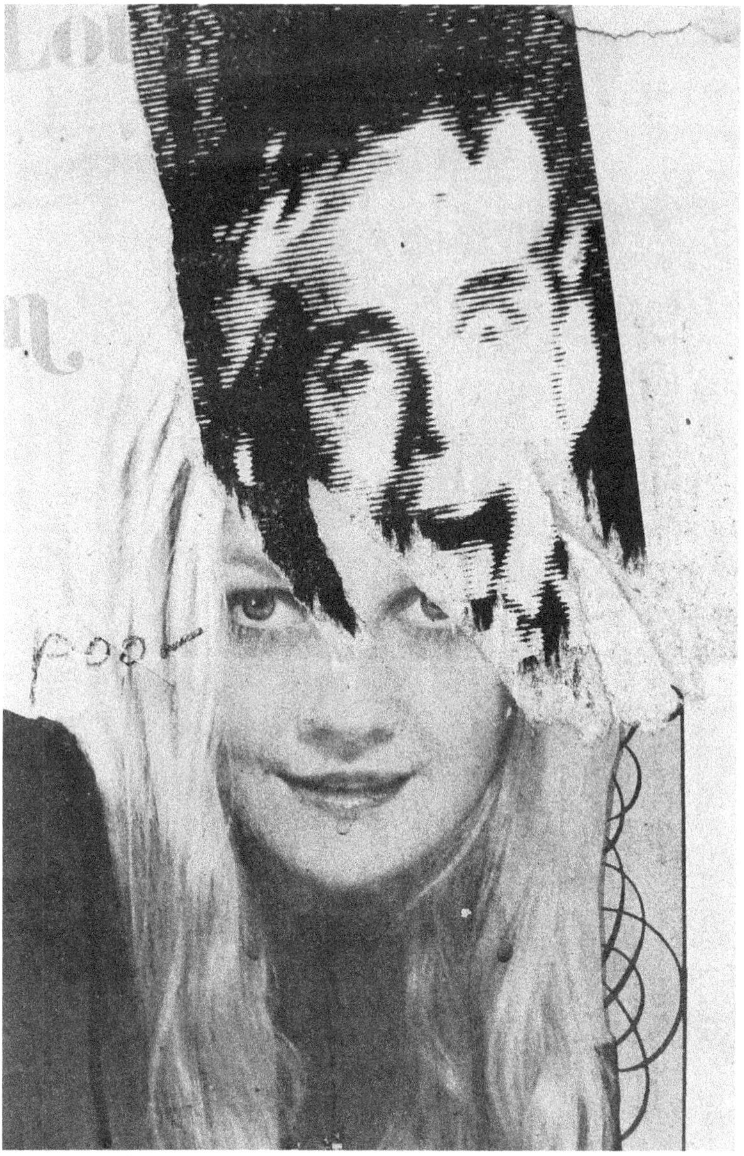
pool

Love's Laissez-Faire Dilettante

The flesh flits from blonde to brunette
like some antique revolving carousel,
one bounds after nymphs, sprites
anxious to stroke each gorgeous, fleeting pore,
while the sky shimmers petulantly
above a just disturbed virgin's pool—
first twittering lemon,
then passionate tangerine,
at last gasping grape.

You linger in secondary, indirect ripples,
(any uncorseted angle will do),
perfection knows not the mandorla or nimbus,
but is subcut into baguette facets—
freckled, bronze, or pale—
rigid belts of striation
are rounded off or tipped about the edges,
heads frenetically bite kaleidoscopic tails
in spring-action, ouroboros-entangled adulterous coils.

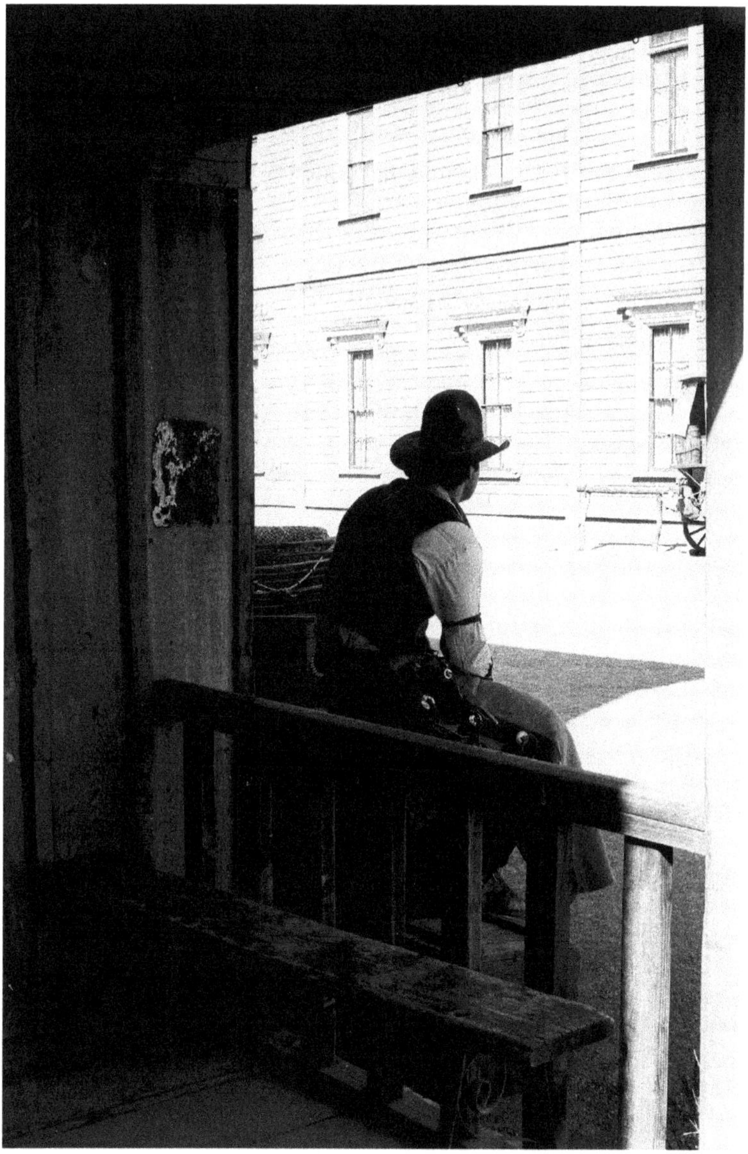

An Old West Advertisement

Mail Order Brides

Companions for those Long, Lonesome Nights

Reproduction Wonders

Guaranteed to Please*

Pictures Tell Only Half the Story

*Sorry, opened merchandise cannot be returned.
Simply discard and reorder.

Listing of Photographs

1. Young woman in antique photo [An Old, Crinkled Treasure Chest]
2. Man and woman in neighboring windows [A Valentine]
3. Girl on the beach winking [Love's Rags]
4. Photographer and smiling woman in mirror [... how much I love you?]
5. Close-up of female eye [The Abduction]
6. Young woman in folk costume [Lay Siege to a Maiden's Honor]
7. Doorknob and door [Outside Your Door]
8. Bride holding bouquet while sitting in car [Good Juliet]
9. Glass bottles with stoppers [Some Loving Potion]
10. Silhouette of man and woman [Determined Lovers]
11. Woman looking out from balcony [The Song of the Young Brave]
12. Two young ladies at flea market [To Please My Friend]
13. Woman standing against striped wall [After a Hell-Raising]
14. Woman in sunglasses [Critical Likeness]
15. Man and woman arguing on street [Why Don't You Listen?]
16. Woman under metal sculpture [Go Away and Nest Elsewhere?]

Listing of Photographs

17. Bedroom with mirrored lampstand [Last Night]
18. Dolls in wedding dresses [Of a St. Agnes' Night]
19. Woman blowing dandelions [Scamper Away Now, Phoebus]
20. Woman holding head, man nearby [Either This or That]
21. Reflection of lower half of male and female [The Wind Has Turned]
22. Music box with guitar-playing doll and ballerina [The Music Box]
23. Hooded woman walking down staircase [M]
24. Empty rowboat [Tears Are Outlawed]
25. Woman's face in soft light [The Imprint of Love]
26. Close-up of face on gravestone [The Keepsake]
27. Reflection of photographer and woman passing by [A 25-Year-Old Menopause Man]
28. Couple holding each other in boat [My Flaming Meteor]
29. Close-up of baby [How Do They Come?]
30. Doll and monkey on dresser [Baby's Playpen]
31. Two boys behind window bars [A Child's Declaration of Rights]
32. Asian American man holding child [The World According to Da-da]
33. Mother and children looking into mirror [When You're 30]
34. Man walking near bullet glass [My Frenetic Nerves]
35. Black child on train [Hush You, Chil'!]
36. Nude female statue looking into her mirror [Giving Birth]
37. Greek warriors on vase [The Judgment of Paris]
38. Woman knitting [Penelope]
39. Reflection of clouds and trees in water [Echo, the Nymph]
40. Nude female statue near windows [Venus]

Listing of Photographs

41. Female manikin head with scraggly hair [Medea with her Medusa Head]
42. Female manikin with wedding veil [Abram's Quandary]
43. Close-up of female manikin head [Hosea]
44. Candle in lantern [The foolish virgins]
45. Woman sitting near lovers' statue [A la John of the Cross]
46. Two nude female manikins [Two Nude Virgins]
47. Couple talking at the Cloisters [a *Charis* all can partake of]
48. Female manikins in lingerie [Au Naturel]
49. Man reading to woman, inset on metal plate [Satisfying a Poet]
50. Woman talking on phone in doorway [Near Dejection]
51. Stalactites and reflection [The Stone Woman]
52. Bridge and World Trade Towers [Erotic Architecture]
53. Woman among leaves [You, a Gazelle]
54. Nude female statue beneath winged statue [Nakedness in the Morning]
55. Torn advertisement of topless film star [Mermaids on Land?]
56. Mosaic of carousing nudes [The Hollow Suburbs]
57. Male following bikini-clad female [Keep Away from Knives]
58. Reflection of female shadow amid windows [She Entered the Blue, Virginal Sky]
59. Two shadowy figures on boardwalk [Promiscuity]
60. Poster of man with drooling tongue above beautiful girl [Love's Laissez-Faire Dilettante]
61. Cowboy looking into street [An Old West Advertisement]

Works Cited

Alter, Robert. *The Art of Biblical Poetry*. New York: Basic Books, 1987.
———. *Strong as Death Is Love: The Song of Songs, Ruth, Esther, Jonah, and Daniel*. New York: Norton, 2015.
Augustine. *Confessions*. Translated by Henry Chadwick. New York: Oxford University Press, 1992.
Bainton, Roland H. *What Christianity Says About Sex, Love and Marriage*. New York: Association Press, 1957.
Barnstone, Willis, trans. *Greek Lyric Poetry*. New York: Schocken, 1975.
Barth, Karl. *Church Dogmatics, Volume III.1: The Doctrine of Creation*, edited by G.W. Bromiley and T.F. Torrance. London: T&T Clark International, 2004.
———. *Church Dogmatics, Volume III.4: The Doctrine of Creation*, edited by G.W. Bromiley and T.F. Torrance. London: T&T Clark International, 2004.
Bloch, Ariel and Chana Bloch. *The Song of Songs: A New Translation*. New York: Random House, 1995.
Boman, Thorleif. *Hebrew Thought Compared with Greek*. Translated by Jules L. Moreau. New York: Norton, 1970.
Carmi, T., ed. and trans. *The Penguin Book of Hebrew Verse*. New York: Penguin, 1981.
Carrier, Constance, trans. *The Poems of Tibullus*. Bloomington: Indiana University Press, 1968.
Delanty, Gregg and Michael Matto, eds. *The Word Exchange: Anglo-Saxon Poems in Translation*. New York: Norton, 2011.
De Rougemont, Denis. *Love in the Western World*. Translated by Montgomery Belgion. New York: Harper & Row, 1974.
Empson, William. *Some Versions of Pastoral*. Norfolk, CT: New Directions, 1960.
Falk, Marcia. *The Song of Songs: A New Translation and Interpretation*. New York: HarperCollins, 1990.
Ferguson, John. *Encyclopedia of Mysticism and Mystery Religions*. New York: Crossroad, 1982.
Flores, Angel, ed. *An Anthology of Spanish Poetry: From Garcilaso to Garcia Lorca*. Garden City, NY: Doubleday, 1961.
Foster, Benjamin R. *Before the Muses: An Anthology of Akkadian Literature, Volume II: Mature, Late*. Bethesda, MD: CDL Press, 1993.

Works Cited

Foster, John L. "Love Poetry: Egyptian." In *The Princeton Handbook of Poetic Terms*, edited by T.V.F. Brogan, 169–70. Princeton: Princeton University Press, 1994.
Foster, Leonard, ed. *The Penguin Book of German Verse*. Baltimore: Penguin, 1959.
Fox, Michael V. *The Song of Songs and the Ancient Egyptian Love Songs*. Madison: University of Wisconsin Press, 1985.
Gardner, Helen, ed. *A Book of Religious Verse*. New York: Oxford University Press, 1972.
———. *The Metaphysical Poets*. Rev. ed. Baltimore: Penguin, 1970.
Gottwald, N.K. "Song of Songs." In *The Interpreter's Dictionary of the Bible, Volume 4*, edited by George Arthur Buttrick, 420–26. Nashville: Abingdon, 1962.
Greer, Rowan A. *Theodore of Mopsuestia, Exegete and Theologian*. London: Faith Press, 1961.
Grierson, H. C. J. "Metaphysical Poetry." In *Seventeenth Century English Poetry*, edited by William R. Keast, 3–21. New York: Oxford University Press, 1962.
Hadas, Moses, trans. *Three Greek Romances*. Indianapolis: Bobbs-Merrill, 1953.
Hardy, Thomas. *Jude the Obscure*. New York: Bantam, 1981.
Haupt, Paul. *The Book of Canticles: A New Rhythmical Translation: With Restoration of the Hebrew Text and Explanatory and Critical Notes*. Chicago: University of Chicago Press, 1902.
Herder, Johann Gottfried von. *Lieder der Liebe: Die Altesten und Schonsten aus dem Morgenlande*. Leipzig: Weygandsche, 1778.
Jasper, David and Stephen Prickett, eds. *The Bible and Literature: A Reader*. Malden, MA: Blackwell, 1999.
Kahane, P. P. *20,000 Years of World Painting, Volume 1: Ancient and Classical Art*, edited by Hans L.C. Jaffe, translated by Robert Erich Wolff. New York: Dell, 1968.
Kavanaugh, Kieran and Otilio Rodriguez, trans. *The Collected Works of St. John of the Cross*. Rev. ed. Washington, DC: ICS Publications, 1991.
Keel, Othmar. *The Song of Songs: A Continental Commentary*. Translated by Frederick J. Gaiser. Minneapolis: Fortress, 1994.
Lewis, C. S. *The Four Loves*. New York: Harcourt Brace Jovanovich, 1960.
Long, G. A. "Song of Songs 2: Ancient Near Eastern Background." In *Dictionary of the Old Testament: Wisdom, Poetry & Writings*, edited by Tremper Longman III and Peter Enns, 750–60. Downers Grove, IL: InterVarsity, 2008.
Mace, David and Vera. *Marriage: East & West*. Garden City, NY: Doubleday, 1960.
MacLean, Hugh, ed. *Edmund Spenser's Poetry*. New York: Norton, 1968.
Maslow, Abraham. "Love in Healthy People." In *The Practice of Love*, edited by Ashley Montague, 89–113. Englewood Cliffs, NJ: Prentice-Hall, 1975.
Murphy, Roland E. *The Song of Songs*, edited by S. Dean McBride, Jr. Minneapolis: Fortress, 1990.
Nahson, Daniel Luis. *The Song of Songs: Fray Luis de Leon's Spanish translation of and commentary on the original biblical text in Hebrew*. Ann Arbor: UMI Dissertation Services, 1996.
Origen. *The Song of Songs: Commentary and Homilies*. Translated by R.P. Lawson. New York: Paulist, 1957.
Paglia, Camille. "Love Poetry: Western." In *The Princeton Handbook of Poetic Terms*, edited by T.V.F. Brogan, 164–69. Princeton: Princeton University Press, 1994.
Plato. *The Dialogues of Plato, Volume 1*. 3rd ed. Translated by Benjamin Jowett, 559–63. London: Oxford University Press, 1892.

Works Cited

Rolle, Richard. *The Fire of Love*. Translated into modern English by Clifton Wolters. Baltimore: Penguin, 1972.

Ryken, Leland, et al., eds. "Sex," "Song of Songs." In *Dictionary of Biblical Imagery*, 776–79; 806–07. Downers Grove, IL: InterVarsity, 1998.

Scheindlin, Raymond P. *The Gazelle: Medieval Hebrew Poems on God, Israel, and the Soul*. Philadelphia: Jewish Publication Society, 1991.

Simpson, William Kelly, ed. *The Literature of Ancient Egypt: An Anthology of Stories, Instructions, and Poetry*. New ed. New Haven: Yale University Press, 1977.

———. *The Literature of Ancient Egypt: An Anthology of Stories, Instructions, Stelae, Autobiographies, and Poetry*. 3rd ed. New Haven: Yale University Press, 2003.

Stallsworthy, Jon, ed. *The Penguin Book of Love Poetry*. New York: Penguin, 1979.

Tannahill, Reay. *Sex in History*. New York: Stein and Day, 1981.

Thompson, Colin B. "*Spiritual Canticle*." *The Westminster Dictionary of Christian Spirituality*, edited by Gordon S. Wakefield, 358–59. Philadelphia: Westminster, 1983.

Weems, Renita J. "Song of Songs." In *The Women's Bible Commentary*, edited by Carol A. Newsome and Sharon H. Ringe, 156–60. Louisville: Westminster/John Knox, 1992.

Whitman, Walt. *Complete Poetry and Selected Prose*, edited by James E. Miller, Jr. Boston: Houghton Mifflin, 1959.

Wiseman, James A., trans. *John Ruusbroec: The Spiritual Espousals and Other Works*. Mahwah, NJ: Paulist, 1985.